D0883982

Suspense
in the Cinema

SUSPENSE
IN THE CINEMA

GORDON GOW

CASTLE BOOKS – NEW YORK

nowledgements

STILLS are reproduced by courtesy of The Academy Cinemas Columbia, Contemporary, M-G-M, Miracle, Nordisk Tonefilm, Orb, Paramount, Planet, Rank, 20th Century-Fox, Unifrance, Allen Eyles, Barrie Pattison, Robin Wood, L'Avant-Scène, and the magazine *films and filming* (Robin Bean).

The quotations marked * are taken from tape recorded interviews made by the author and broadcast in BBC programmes. Most of them were published subsequently in *films and filming*. The quotations from Claude Chabrol in Chapter 2 and from Louis Malle in Chapter 8 are from articles published in *films and filming*.

Library of Congress Catalog Card No.: 68–15196

This Edition Published by Arrangement
With A. S. Barnes & Co., Inc.

Printed in the United States of America

To
Joyce and Stephen

Contents

1. Introduction

SUSPENSE is a familiar condition, brought on by life. Workaday existence can easily become a survival contest, waged in the cheerless shadow of world events. The communication media keep us in touch with matters we might be disinclined to touch with a ten-foot pole; yet curiosity and conscience, mixed in varying proportions, decree that we must be aware of such things. So the latest news is on tap, very properly. One of the tricks of survival is to avoid swallowing it in massive doses.

The big trouble with day-to-day news is that it's a collection of unfinished anecdotes. It leaves questions hovering: will a war be waged? will a murderer be apprehended? will taxes increase? will tea stain the lining of the stomach and (as a letter to *The Times* once demanded) "if so does it matter?" Before the answers are known, days or even months can elapse, by which time other questions have arisen to claim priority in our crowded areas of awareness. Thus the chronic imbiber of news will live in perpetual suspense.

"Welcome to Milltown, A Very Nervous Little Community": so reads the sign that fills the screen at the beginning of *The Ladies Man* (1961, directed by Jerry Lewis). Doubtless a town in touch with the news. The camera rises above the sign, disclosing a sedate square and a solitary woman who makes her way along a footpath and crosses a street. Her edgy demeanour signifies at once that she is a typical Milltown inhabitant. For this reason, the empty streets hold a quiet menace. One senses that, although the town looks ordinary, at any moment some frightfulness will break forth. So it does. The nervous woman, having crossed the road safely but evidently feeling none the better for that,

9

continues along past shopfronts where the stillness of Milltown is sharply disrupted by a man who enters the frame suddenly and bids her a hearty "Good morning." The woman screams as if assaulted, and flattens herself in terror against a shop window. Her scream is the cue for a swift proliferation of calamities. Citizens of Milltown rush into view. One of them overturns a parrot cage outside a pet shop: the parrot screeches. A grocer, crossing the street, upsets his load of canned food. A car stops with a squeal of tyres. A boy riding past on a bicycle, twirling to dodge the chaos, crashes into a telephone pole, which vibrates, causing a workman on top of the pole to slide down it, impaling himself on a spike.

Here, in a manner that is essentially filmic, we have a salutary and hilarious heightening of life, and at the same time an explanation of why people seek suspense in the cinema. Drawn there by the boredom of routine lives that are subjected to the pressures that nag at the nerves, they find release in the exaggeration, consolation in the fact that "it's only a film", and at the same time, since the most extreme of films can be related to life, they recognise their own fears writ large and are partially purged.

2. Precepts

CINEMA is a medium that can induce suspense more readily than any other. It might be argued that many films, and certainly the majority of those mentioned in this book, have derived their plots and ideas from novels. But the images and sounds of cinema are another language: a transformation is wrought: the ideas impinge in a different manner, and more strongly. For no matter how deep a spell the written word may cast, none but the recluse can surrender completely. Any number of things will intervene: conversa-

10

tion, telephone, food, and even work, will demand that the thread be snapped repeatedly. The same goes for television, and for movies viewed at home. The stage comes nearest to cinema in holding attention, because the audience has fore-gathered with the communal disposition to watch and listen for a couple of hours, and will usually contrive to do so even when the atmosphere is less than ideal. In matters of suspense, however, the cinema still has the advantage over theatre, on account of its more flexible technique. If a murder is to be committed on the stage, and the identity of the murderer is to be kept secret from the audience until the end of the play, there must be a great deal of contrivance with lighting or disguises of one kind or another. The cinema can show merely the killer's hands or feet, close to camera, and thereby impart the ultimate in tension and mystery. The door that opens slowly, with or without a creak, can be preceded in the cinema by a close-up of the disquieting doorknob, slowly turning: a detail that a spectator at a stage performance, seated perhaps at the back of the stalls, could hardly be expected to see.

So the ability to change viewpoint quite arbitrarily, with rhythmic or abrupt cutting as the occasion requires, and to restrict or expand the range of vision, gives the film director great control over the spectator's response. Consider that doorknob: a traditional element of suspense cinema, a har-binger of doom or of anti-climactic relief. It does yeoman duty in Don Siegel's *The Verdict* (1946), a moderate think-thriller made in the U.S.A. but set in Victorian London with plenty of fog.

The doorknob sequence of *The Verdict* begins when Mrs. Benson (Rosalind Ivan), a landlady very much on edge because a murder has been committed in her house and the killer is still at large, informs one of the lodgers, Victor Emmric (Peter Lorre), who has come home rather late at night, that he would do well to follow her example and wear a whistle on a string around his neck in case somebody breaks into his bedroom. Victor, who might for all we know at this point of the story be the murderer himself, remarks that once your throat is cut you cannot blow a whistle, and Mrs. Benson scurries nervously down to her basement room. Victor

11

mounts the stairs, singing a mildly bawdy song. He pauses to
light a candle from a bracket on the landing, and then blows
the other candles out, deepening the shadows, and goes on up
to his room. Now the camera is positioned inside Victor's
room, which is in darkness that is not much alleviated when he
opens the door and enters. We have time to wonder if somebody is lurking in the darkness before Victor lights the gas
and we see that he is quite alone. He takes a gun from his
pocket and puts it on the bedside table. Now there is a cut to
Mrs. Benson's room. She is in bed. A cat lies on the covers beside her. She laces her glass of milk with brandy, fingers the
police whistle that dangles from her neck, and picks up a
luridly illustrated magazine that has an article about the
murderer who is so much on her mind. This does her no good,
but she does get to sleep, and the cat laps at her unfinished
glass of milk and brandy, and hiccups.

Given these conditions, we are confronted by the first
doorknob, the one on the inside of Victor's bedroom door.
Victor seems to be sleeping when our attention is drawn to
the doorknob (or, to be precise, door handle, for it is rather
an elegant thing in itself). Beneath it, Victor's key, with a
chain dangling from it, remains in the keyhole where he left
it, but as we watch it is pushed out by somebody on the other
side of the door. At once there is a big close-up of Victor's
face, his eyes flicker and he wakes up. He sees the door
sneaking open, and around the edge of the door creeps a
black-gloved hand. As Victor reaches for the gun on the
bedside table, the camera observes him from across the table
and begins a slightly circling movement which serves the
double purpose of taking the table away from the centre of
the screen and pacing the tension as Victor levels the gun.
He fires. The black-gloved hand disappears from the door.
Victor runs out on to the landing and fires down into the
darkness of the staircase.

The second doorknob (which is indubitably a knob) is in
the basement room occupied by Mrs. Benson, who has been
awakened by the shots and now beholds her doorknob
twisting back and forth. Her fear is such that she cannot
summon the breath to blow her whistle. However, in line with

the tradition of anti-climax, it is only Victor at her door: our suspicion of him has been removed, for the moment, because we feel that the black-gloved hand must have been the murderer's. Cunningly, however, doubt is raised again, when we see the principal character of the film, a man named Grodman (Sydney Greenstreet), returning hurriedly to his house directly opposite. He has black gloves which fall to the floor and are closely and swiftly noted by the camera. This makes it clear that Grodman was the intruder at Victor's door. What is not clear is whether Grodman's intrusion was for the purpose of gathering evidence against Victor, or whether Grodman himself is the killer. We know Grodman is seeking to unravel the mystery, and we know better than to trust our impulsive response to the black gloves. So we suspect Victor again.

In this state of doubt, we are confronted by a third door-knob in Mrs. Benson's house, and around the door comes another black-gloved hand. Mrs. Benson registers great alarm, but the hand in the glove belongs to an anti-climactic police superintendent.

These jollities, neatly controlled within the framework of a mainly sober melodrama, are typical of cinematic suspense. They rely upon the ability of film to direct our attention and our powers of reasoning. We look at doorknobs in close-up. We observe the reactions of faces. We mark the enigmatic black gloves. The suspense is timed, by camera movement and by cutting, to increase steadily, engaging our concern. At the same time, the comic ingredients of the whistle and the cat and the landlady serve to modify our involvement, affording us a superior smile. Consequently, with our emotions tolerably restrained, our minds can flex themselves. Don Siegel provided in this sequence an object lesson in balance, giving equal weight to the *frissons* of suspense and the diverting cerebral activity of trying to guess the culprit.

Simultaneously, *The Verdict* raised psychological and ethical problems. Grodman, a richly idiosyncratic study by Greenstreet, is an ex-superintendent of police, who, having been mistakenly responsible for the execution of an innocent man, corrects his mistake in retirement by discovering and

13

killing the real murderer, thereby becoming a murderer himself.

Precepts for the efficient cutting in this film date well back into the history of cinema. Arthur Knight, in his book *The Liveliest Art*, records that a familiar principle, cross-cutting for a peril-and-rescue sequence, was employed by D. W. Griffith as early as 1909 in *The Lonely Villa* for a passage that alternated between shots of a mother shielding her children against rogues who had broken in, and shots of the father driving against time to the aid of his family. "By cutting back and forth from one to the other," writes Knight, "making each shot shorter than the last, Griffith heightened the excitement of the situation."

Cutting for suspense is invariably keen when the spectator has been alerted to a danger that the potential victim knows nothing about. This is a durable precept, expertly observed and refreshed in the opening sequence of *Robbery* (1967, directed by Peter Yates). A getaway car, pursued closely by a police car, is speeding through London streets, recklessly, swerving and mounting kerbs, taking corners wildly. Fast cross-cutting from getaway car to police car maintains a high pulse-rate until, abruptly, there is a cut to something ironically placid. At a section of road that lies ahead, school children have gathered in orderly fashion on the footpath and are proceeding to cross the street. The spectator knows what they do not, and quite possibly his palms are sweating. Cutting is also the essential partner of realism when the getaway car seems to plough right through them.

But if suspense is mounting slowly and insidiously, the absence of cutting (or, by means of crafty elisions in the editing, the apparent absence of it) can be a virtue, giving place to the flowing camera movement that leads the spectator into the environment. Camera mobility can be extended by the use of model scenery placed in the foreground and movable, so that the camera can endow us with powers of levitation, leading us through a window and on into a room. The exterior of the building, with the window, being near the camera, creates a false perspective. It is also, perhaps, split down the middle, ready to be snatched out of the way once

14

the camera has gone through the window, thus leaving the field free for continued camera movement inside the room. A notable elaboration of the mobile view is allied, at the beginning of John Farrow's *The Big Clock* (1947), to the old anxiety-device of starting with a situation that belongs chronologically near the end of the story. We see a man in a certain mysterious predicament, and then in flashback we are shown what led to it. A foretaste of thrills in store will possibly maintain our interest in the exposition of the plot, which might otherwise seem dull. *The Big Clock* begins with a panning shot across a city skyline by night, moving in on a tall office building and taking us through a window and into a corridor where a man (Ray Milland) is lurking as though anxious to hide. The camera follows him as he moves stealthily along the corridor and then up a curving staircase and into a circular room which contains the machinery of a large clock. Still on the move, while the soundtrack gives voice to the man's thoughts, the camera encircles the clock-room with him and then centres upon his face in close-up as he looks out through an opening in the wall. In this position, the camera draws back from the man's face, transporting us through the barrier of the wall, so that we see the man virtually caged inside the clock. Now we move across to the face of the clock. Here the flow of movement is temporarily halted. There is a dissolve, to the same clock face showing an earlier time. The flashback (the film proper) has begun.

Techniques of suspense have become as much a part of the language of cinema as the more fundamental assets of westerns. The western is held to be indigenous cinema on account of the pictorial value of wide open spaces, plus the fact that, as John Wayne once remarked, "of all the things that can move in the movies, nothing will *appear* to move more than the horse".* But all westerns must add the techniques of suspense. Time and again the dirt street of the little western town is cleared for the climax. The street is empty, save for the two men who are approaching one another, stealthily, suspensefully, down the length of it. Presently they will be close enough to perform the familiar *pliés* as they reach for

15

their guns. The set-up has passed beyond the category of the hackneyed, and into tradition. No matter how often it is repeated, the *cinéphile* will never tire of it.

Of course, daunting precepts have been established by those much-chronicled masters of tension, Fritz Lang and Alfred Hitchcock. It was Lang who stopped cars at traffic lights in *Das Testament des Dr. Mabuse* (1933), and, in a memorable overhead shot when the lights changed again, had all the cars move off except one—because during that short halt the driver had been murdered. It was Hitchcock who sent a woman to Robert Donat's bedroom in *The Thirty-nine Steps* (1935), to move equivocally toward him and then pitch forward across his legs to reveal the dagger embedded in her back. And, when the talkies were new, both Lang and Hitchcock realised that they were good for more than merely talking: thus Peter Lorre, in Lang's *M* (1931), whistles a snatch of "In the Hall of the Mountain King" to convey to the audience that murder is on his mind; and in Hitchcock's *Blackmail* (1929) a girl obsessed by thoughts of a knife murder overhears a conversation in which words become blurred, except for one word, repeated and becoming louder each time, the word "knife". Variations on this use of sound for menace, directly or subjectively, have become as indigenous to suspense as the visuals. In the George Stevens version of Theodore Dreiser's novel *An American Tragedy* (*A Place in the Sun*, 1951), the cry of a loon is heard among the shadowy trees surrounding Loon Lake, as George Eastman (Montgomery Clift) rows Alice Tripp (Shelley Winters) in a small boat, deeper into the darkness, intending to murder her and then weakening in resolve. The cry has been heard before, in daylight, when George was told of a death by drowning in the lake and the idea of murder entered his mind for the first time. Now, Alice rises in the row-boat, overturning it, and is drowned accidentally. In long-shot of dark lake and distant boat, the moment is punctuated visually, and also audibly as the loon cries yet again. And later, when George takes the witness stand in court at his trial for murder, the loon cry, loud and subjective, is allied with a close-up of his stricken face.

"Mysterious predicament"—Ray Milland THE BIG CLOCK.

Suspense can be protracted effectively if the situation is strong. Ingmar Bergman, whose films contain many examples of traditional suspense technique, provides a classic illustration of this toward the end of *Jungfrukällan* (*The Virgin Spring*, 1959), when a father (Max von Sydow) has the upper hand of the men who raped and killed his daughter, and has made up his mind to murder them. His vengeance in itself is reprehensible (this is the major point of the film), and his period of preparation is ruthless. It is dawn. Against a grey sky, the man seizes the slender trunk of a birch-tree, bending it back and forth in controlled and determined rage until it bows to the ground. He uses branches of it for his ritual bath. Deliberately, ironically, his body is prepared for the work ahead. The rapists are asleep in his house. He sits for a long time in the room where they lie, watching them silently. His hate is festering. The long knife is thrust into the wooden table beside him: it stands ready. Outside, a rooster crows. The killing is to be revenged symbolically. The sunlight from the window increases, until the waiting man, resplendent in the light of it, is at the height of his lust, savouring the false sweetness before the self-degradation begins.

17

Cerebral suspense can linger when a film is over: in Henri Colpi's *Une aussi longue absence* (1961), the quiet suspense resides in the attempts of a woman (Alida Valli) to prove that a vagrant (Georges Wilson), who has lost his memory, is really her husband who was captured by the Germans during the war and has long been presumed dead; at the end, when she is virtually convinced that her hopes are justified, the vagrant is frightened and runs away, leaving her to wait for the winter to come and the cold to urge him back . . . perhaps. This film is an essay on memory and communication, more intellectual than emotional, but certainly a film of suspense.

In comedy, emotional suspense is often mocked. Instinctive fears are exaggerated to the point where we laugh at them. Vertigo, for example is a sensation that the film can readily evoke, with or without the safeguard of process shooting, and with or without an acrobat to double for the star. Harold Lloyd's vertiginous gymnastics on a high building in *Safety Last* (1923) and Jean-Paul Belmondo's in *L'homme de Rio* (1964, directed by Philippe de Broca) were carried out on location by the actors themselves. For Lloyd it was a matter of necessity. William Cahn points out in *Harold Lloyd's World of Comedy* that "those were the days before the trick photography and process film development. The illusion lay in the deceptive camera angles of drop in height." Even so, it was dangerous, and more convincing than process shooting.

The extravagant predicament and the exaggerated alarm of the man who teeters on a high ledge and indicates to us that at any moment he might lose his balance and fall will induce a laugh. In a way, this laugh is callous, because the instinct of vertigo is common and we are laughing at somebody who is feeling as bad as we ourselves would feel in a similar position. Yet the object of the exercise is to make us laugh which does us good. Given a vertiginous situation in a serious film we will not laugh, provided the work is persuasive. But comedy often promotes an alienation, a feeling of superiority to the character on the screen, which bolsters the spectator's self-confidence. Laurel and Hardy, in *The Music Box* (1932), haul a piano up a steep flight of steps with notable ineptitude.

We watch in gleeful suspense, knowing that the wretched, thing is apt to slide all the way down again, which it does. Their clumsiness is consoling. We all feel clumsy at times, but how heartening it is to realise that we never have it quite so bad as that. To some degree, at the same moment that we laugh, we sympathise. It would be callous indeed to deny a little fellow-feeling to Buster Keaton when, in *The Navigator* (1924), a glowering and disembodied face moves back and forth at the porthole of his cabin. To him it is an apparition, for beyond the porthole, surely, there is nothing but the sea. We know better. A portrait (of Donald Crisp, who co-directed the film with Keaton) is suspended on the side of the ship and is swaying with the swell of the ocean. Even so, in the superior position of knowing what Keaton doesn't know, we can still understand his fear of the unexpected.

The word "suspense" does not imply a distinct genre, because suspense is as appropriate in a profound film as it is in the lightest of parody-thrillers. It is relevant not only to private eyes and secret agents, but to the class-warring of *The Servant* (directed by Joseph Losey, 1963) or to the implicit questioning of wartime morality in *Orders to Kill*

"Vengeance"—
Max von Sydow in
THE VIRGIN SPRING.   19

(directed by Anthony Asquith, 1957). Most commonly, however, suspense is associated with thrillers, which predominate among the examples in this book, and thrillers are sometimes dismissed by and large as mere entertainments. It is true that many of them aspire no higher, often inciting a levity that their makers do not necessarily intend. Yet even these are capable of flexing the mind. Personally I incline toward the opinion of producer Sam Spiegel that "the best motion pictures are those that reach you as entertainment and that, by the time you leave, have provoked thoughts. A picture that provokes no thoughts is usually not well conceived, and doesn't entertain one anyway."* In regard to thrillers specifically, Claude Chabrol goes so far as to say "No matter how much a scenarist or director may seek to distract, a thriller must be profound, because it speaks of life and death."* And C. A. Lejeune, writing in *The Observer* (November 11, 1946), has defined the appeal of thrillers as "the endlessly fascinating and profitable quest for motive in the odd behaviour of man. It is a very healthy and natural thing to enjoy a thriller . . . in a certain sense, the thriller is the most moral of all stories, because it seeks to discover what has thrown a single mind out of gear."

3. Isolation

THE key figure in a suspense film is very often isolated and vulnerable. This person's dangerous solitude can be evoked quite strongly through the *mise en scène*, and the setting is a major factor, enclosing the potential victim in an atmosphere of latent menace. To take an old-fashioned but resilient example, the 1939 version of *The Hound of the Baskervilles*, directed by Sidney Lanfield, had as its locale a moderately fantasticated Dartmoor. As envisaged and constructed in Hollywood, on the wrong side of realism (which was right enough for the purpose), it was a foggy region of brooding crags and quagmire, a forbidding place even by day, and more so when eerie howls were heard in the night. Remote in the midst of it stood the bleak mansion that had been inherited by young Sir Henry Baskerville (Richard Greene).

The story, derived from Conan Doyle, brings Sir Henry home from Canada in the 1880s to take up his heirdom and with it the legendary curse of a phantom hound that roams the moor by night in quest of Baskerville prey. His immediate predecessor, chased by something unseen, dies of a heart attack on the moor as the film begins. The imputations are nicely divided between a mercenary plot against the family and the hint of metaphysical vengeance for ancient philandering. The young man himself, affluent and fresh of face, is the very picture of security, treating the legend of the hound with

"A hand is at her throat"—Barbara Stanwyck in SORRY, WRONG NUMBER.

"Alone in the lift"—
Olivia de Havilland in LADY IN A CAGE (below with Jeff Corey).

mild disdain. No neurotic, he. It is for other characters in the film, and for the spectator as well, to tremble on his behalf.

With the briskness of the Hollywood thirties, the edgy Dr. Mortimer (Lionel Atwill) outlines the situation in the Baker Street rooms of Sherlock Holmes (Basil Rathbone). The doctor is concerned for Sir Henry. He remarks that all Baskervilles tend to die violently, and that near the spot on the moor where the most recent death occurred there were unusual footprints in the dank earth. Upon being asked what kind of footprints, he promotes an instant *frisson*: "Mr. Holmes, they were the footprints of a gigantic hound."

A decade of sound had taught Hollywood when to rely on dialogue to maintain tension, and when to brace it up with visual reinforcements. Up to that line, the words hold. Now Dr. Mortimer regales Holmes with the legend, which he reads from a tattered old manuscript. (He reads at a very rapid pace. This could be put down to the state of his nerves, but more likely it is due to the fashion of the period. Films of the thirties were much faster than they are now, and proportionately simpler of course; but to look again at one like this, a humdinger of its kind in its own day, is to realise that many suspense films of more recent date are unnecessarily protracted and forfeit a deal of tension on that account.) As Dr. Mortimer reads, the manuscript fills the frame for a moment and then the centre of it becomes an inner screen, blurred at the edges, on which we receive visual impressions of a jaunty Baskerville rake who in years gone by took liberties with village girls until the vengeful hound put an end to his arrogant joy. We see the hound, a big black creature, all eyes and fangs. From the wrong side of realism, then, we have been led willingly to the verge of fantasy.

Down a little nearer to earth, Dr. Mortimer and young Sir Henry walk the night streets of London, followed slowly by a hansom cab with curtained windows. A close view shows us a hand with a gun emerging from the curtain. Before Sir Henry can be shot, Holmes approaches along the footpath and warns him. The cab moves quickly away. Two suspenseful possibilities hover: a mythical dog or a man with a gun.

23

From one or the other Sir Henry is in peril.

The next *frisson* to note is one of those doorknobs. Dr. Watson (Nigel Bruce), is occupying a room in the Baskerville mansion in order to keep an eye on things for Holmes, who is supposed to be still in London (actually, he isn't). Watson is penning a dutiful letter to him, mostly about the sinister feel of the place, when a small sound causes him to glance at the door. In close-up the door handle is turned very slowly. The anti-climax follows fast: it is only Sir Henry who enters.

Sir Henry, in bounding health, is forever striding forth into the fog that shrouds his domain. He is warned by all, with the exception of one John Stapleton (Morton Lowry), who expresses the opinion that a weird howl from the distance "could be the wind, or a bittern booming". Bittern is a splendid word to use (in fact, Stapleton uses it again in another scene) because, although such a bird exists, it sounds unlikely and breeds doubt. Not every line of the dialogue is felicitous, however. There is an unfortunate utterance by Sir Henry, after a dinner party at the Stapleton house on the other side of the moor, when he declines a ride home and faces the darkness and fog with "It's such a beautiful night, I think I'll walk." What follows, though, is a classic of suspenseful cross-cutting, the chase at its choicest. First the villain is disclosed to us. He lets loose a sizeable hound from a vault on the moor, waves a boot stolen from Sir Henry in front of the beast's nostrils, and thereby causes it to leap from its lair with the power and lightness of a good Siegfried springing from the wings for the coda of the Black Swan *pas de deux*. Now comes the back-and-forth cutting from Sir Henry, dapper in his expensive overcoat and scarf, walking purposefully through the fog, to the hounding beast, lithe and swift in pursuit. When the familiar howl is heard (improbably, perhaps, from a hound given his freedom to run), Sir Henry stops in his tracks, looks rather disturbed, and proceeds at a sharper pace. The cross-cutting grows faster, of course, as the hound gains ground, the soundtrack registers his panting, and at last Sir Henry begins to run. In this traditional and infallible manner, suspense builds until, with perfect timing, we reach the first shot in which man and dog appear together. The attack, relying upon the deception that quick cutting permits, is very persuasive. The struggle between man and man-sized dog leaves Sir Henry credibly mauled.

Very soon after this, there is another opportunity for cross-cutting. Sensibly, it is not taken. Although the situation is different, a case of peril and rescue rather than a chase, judgement has been keen and stylistic repetition is avoided. Sherlock Holmes (who has been hanging around the moor disguised as an old goat) has seen to the immediate safety of Sir Henry after the hound's attack. Now he goes dashing off to find clues, and discovers the vault where the hound has been kept. Holmes is rash enough to jump into the vault. Immediately the lid comes thundering down on top of him and the villain applies the lock. The obvious thing here would have been to cut away to Sir Henry's predicament, for he is in further danger now, not from the hound but from the human. But first we linger for a second or two in the vault with Holmes, as he takes a clasp knife from his pocket and goes to work. After this, without cross-cuts, we know that he is trying to come to the rescue, and our attention is given over entirely to Sir Henry, who is back at home, weak and swathed in bandages, in the company of the man we know to be the villain. This man sends the housekeeper out of the room to fetch hot water or something like that, and then, under the guise of friendship, hands Sir Henry a glass of sedative, potent enough to put him to sleep forever. While we are aware that Holmes is doing his best, we have no guarantee, other than cynicism, that he will succeed. The glass is in Sir Henry's hand and almost to his lips before the door bursts open, and Holmes strides into the room to dash the glass to the floor.

In addition to the precision of its technique, the fascination of this film lies in its gathering of tension through atmosphere and plot while the demeanour of the key figure, Sir Henry, goes firmly against the grain. A straightforward, one-dimensional leading man type, he treats the palpable menace in the foggy air as little more than an irritation, so far removed from his usual experience of life that he cannot bring himself to be bothered by it. This is not a fault in the actor, but in the policies of a period that saw leading men as handsome ciphers. More frequently, the person in danger was a woman; once a cipher too, whose fate was to be tied to railroad tracks and to be rescued before the train quite reached her. Her troubles soon became psychological as well as physical. In the cinema of suspense, her fear is often with us. So is the compulsion, greater than fear, which bids her investigate noises in the night, alone, isolated, vulnerable, and clad in something frail, usually a nightdress, risking the possible threats of draught, dew, candle flame and clutching paws. Hare-brained, of course, but not unrelated to human emotions. Fear breeds a compulsion to know the worst. Cinematically, this familiar excursion is capable of refinement. In *Paranoiac* (1964, directed by Freddie Francis), Eleanor (Janette Scott) goes out into the garden of a house in the country at night, because she has seen from her bedroom window somebody-down-there who looks like her long-dead brother. Although she carries neither candle nor torch, she moves through the dark garden in a circle of light which is diffused at its periphery. In the circumstances, this modification of the brash theatrical spotlight is rather daring. It places stylised emphasis upon her isolation, and heightens the potential menace of the dimly-seen shrubbery beyond the pool of light. It reflects her state of mind as well, perhaps: the feeling that she is all too visible to anybody who might be lurking in the bushes.

Freddie Francis had used the same effect before when he was lighting cameraman on Jack Clayton's *The Innocents* (1961). There, the governess (Deborah Kerr), lured by the sensual whispers of ghosts, moves through corridors and down a staircase, and the light from her candle seems to contain itself strangely within a circle. It was for this occasion that Francis had filters made, which were subtle variations on the single-colour filters often used in black-and-white photography. (A red filter, for example, will turn a blue sky dark, so that a scene happening ostensibly at night can be shot outdoors in the daytime.) The Francis filters have a clear area (the pool of light), but toward the outer edges there is a range of colour, merging delicately from yellow to dark red. Attached to the camera, these filters permit one clear area of light beyond which there will be underexposed areas of increasing darkness. "It would have been a very long job to achieve this by studio lighting," says Francis, "because the camera had to move, and the concentrated area of light had to move with the governess."

As a matter of passing interest, the filters were actually made in a cottage at Chalfont St. Giles by an elderly woman living and working alone, with a small dog for company: a bemusing thought to set against the factory image of commercial film production. Ever since *The Innocents,* these filters have often been borrowed by other film-makers. Apart from their contribution to mood, they are a means of masking portions of the CinemaScope frame, or frames of equivalent shape.

A number of imaginative directors have met the challenge of the elongated screens with methods prefigured by Griffith when he black-masked certain shots in the silent days, confining a detailed image to a circle or a triangle. A sprightly elaboration of this rudimentary idea can be found in the films of Sidney J. Furie, who is a great one for splitting a composition into segments. In both *The Ipcress File* (1965) and *The Naked Runner* (1967), one of Furie's most notable effects is to exaggerate the familar principle of over-shoulder shooting. When a man is figuratively "in a tight corner", the greater part of the big oblong frame is filled by the looming shoulder of the person who has him cornered. Most of the screen is masked by shoulder, while the face (be it that of Michael Caine or Frank Sinatra) is confined to the top-left hand corner of the screen in metaphorical isolation.

A sense of isolation can prevail, ironically, in a crowded city. Such is the case in Anatole Litvak's film of Lucille Fletcher's *Sorry, Wrong Number* (1948). A wealthy woman, Leona Stevenson (Barbara Stanwyck) is partially paralysed, and bed-ridden; her condition is psychosomatic. She is alone at night in the bedroom of her house in New York, because earlier her husband (Burt Lancaster) told the nurse and servants that they could have the night off. But now her husband has not returned from the office. Telephoning to find out why, Leona gets a crossed line and overhears two men talking about a murder which one of them has been paid to commit later in the night, on behalf of a husband who is eager to be rid of his wife and in possession of her money. Not realising, or not permitting herself to suspect, that she is the potential victim, Leona spends an hysterical few hours on the telephone, sounding increasingly neurotic, and failing to persuade the police, or her doctor, or anybody else, that what she says is true. At the hour mentioned by the murderer on the crossed line, Leona hears somebody mounting the stairs toward her bedroom. The telephone rings. It is her husband, who has changed his mind and wants to prevent the killing. But Leona has dropped the telephone. It dangles on its cord. A hand is at her throat. The intruder does what he was paid to do, and, before replacing the telephone receiver, says into it, "Sorry, wrong number."

The contrived melodrama is rich in detail and in irony. Leona's wealth does not provide security in her crisis. Her house is in a heavily populated city, but people are unaware of her danger. The impersonal nature of the city is against her. The telephone, a mechanical irritant, affords no true communication. At the same time, these thoughts are aggravated by Leona's personal state of mind. She is her own worst enemy, believing, against medical opinion to the contrary, that she is physically incapable of moving from her bed.

The film was adapted by Lucille Fletcher from her radio play of the same name, a celebrated and rare example of drama written strictly for the ear, nervy with telephone voices and telephone noises. The cinema's longer version was flawed by the familiar (and usually valid) process of opening-out, which took us away from Leona in her bedroom to change the scene and pad the running time, breaking the enclosed tension. At shorter length, perhaps half an hour, it could have been a tighter and more suspenseful essay in close-range technique.

A similar basic point, about the unwillingness of city dwellers to shed their anonymity and become involved, is made in a more concentrated fashion in Walter Grauman's *Lady in a Cage* (1964). The woman (Olivia de Havilland) has a bad hip.

28

"Five cellars deep" —
Lon Chaney and Mary Philbin in
THE PHANTOM OF THE OPERA.

29

A lift has been installed in the house to carry her back and forth between the ground floor and the landing at the top of the stairs. During a hot weekend, she is alone and in the lift, when it sticks halfway, and, while she is thus caged, a number of ill-disposed people enter the house.

The suspense tactics are often keen. The first intruder, a drunk, makes noises that she welcomes as a token of rescue near at hand, but a sudden zoom (from her elevated viewpoint down to the glaring eye of the drunk) changes her relief into fear. When she opens the doors of her lift and tries to struggle and squirm and let herself fall, our sympathy is with her. Out of her own mouth come words that take sympathy away. She writes poetry, not very well, and she is a snob. Both these factors combine when she describes another intruder, a delinquent with a stocking mask distorting his face, as "one of the bits of offal thrown up by the welfare state". The trouble is that such utterances also break the tension. The violence of the younger intruders serves to strip away her facade of culture and reduce her to the primitive, which is a fair enough way of suggesting the animal that lurks within civilised humans, but, as she arms herself, she says "Stone age, here I come." Probably, being the woman she is, and driven to such distress, this is exactly what she would say, yet dramatically it is too much. Some moderation of the dialogue would have helped immeasurably.

Where Grauman makes his point most strongly is in the spare impressions he gives us of the outside world. The weather is oppressive. Heat accentuates the common apathy. Nobody pays any attention to the emergency bell that rings outside the house when the woman presses a button in the lift. Even when the violent action is carried to its conclusion on the sidewalk in front of the house, with a slow stream of traffic passing by, it is quite some time before notice is taken.

It is interesting that the physical disabilities of the women in *Sorry, Wrong Number* and *Lady in a Cage* are not lightly used as mere springboards for suspense, but are as relevant to the moral issues as they are to the melodrama. By comparison, there is a touch of glibness to the way a physical handicap is pressed into the service of melodrama in Robert Siodmak's *The Spiral Staircase* (1945). The heroine, Helen

(Dorothy McGuire), is dumb. She is the prey of an unknown murderer who has been killing a number of physically disabled girls in a small New England town. In the long run, largely on account of Dorothy McGuire's beautifully judged performance and her ability to keep a tight rein on pathos, the film does manage (despite itself?) to symbolise the lack of communication among humans which has been explored more conscientiously in certain films of the 1960s. Even more glib is the attitude toward the murderer's insanity. He kills (God help us) to destroy imperfection, which is in his opinion too offensive to be tolerated. No time is taken to make the appropriate point about adjustment to the imperfections of life. Helen's climactic shock restores her voice, and the villain is despatched by a bullet and dismissed with the vengeful cry of "Murderer" (from his mother). This is the "mad-and-good-riddance" policy that has done so much to earn thrillers a bad name.

Indignation does not blind me to the splendours of the *mise en scène*, however, because *The Spiral Staircase* is rich both in visual effect and in the precise employment of suspense techniques. The period of the story is 1906, and the opening sequence shows Helen weeping in sympathy over the dead heroine of a silent movie which is being projected in the darkened parlour of a local hotel, while, in one of the bedrooms above, a girl who is physically deformed is being murdered. Helen, who works as a housemaid in a beautifully brooding mansion a little way out of town, walks back as night falls and a storm begins. Conscious of her own vulnerability, she approaches the house in trepidation, picking up a twig and rattling it along the railings to comfort herself with sound. The thunder and lightning are going strong as she moves through the gate and walks across the garden. A tree is in the foreground of the frame, at the left, while Helen is seen beyond it, moving from left to right. Suddenly, a great flash of lightning throws into relief the silhouette of a man who stands by the tree. Helen does not see him. She goes on into the house, and, halfway up the stairs, she pauses on a landing to look at herself in a mirror. She touches her mouth. On a higher landing, looking down toward her, is a man, most probably the same one who was lurking in the garden.

We see his feet, and then an enormous close-up of one of his eyes in which Helen's face is subjectively reflected: the mouth misted, obliterated. These things are splendid in themselves; but one must reach far to pluck significance, with welcome aid from Dorothy McGuire in respect of the physical disability which can be seen as a heightened form of inadequacy: a condition known to most of us in varying degrees and from time to time.

The point is better made within Henri-Georges Clouzot's comic-macabre thriller *Les Espions* (1957), where another dumb woman (played by Véra Clouzot) is among the patients of a spy-ridden psychiatric clinic. She overhears something disturbing and is anxious to communicate the information, but is quite unable to make herself understood.

The suspense, in a grotesque ambiance, still permits a valid concern for the woman as she vents her frustration. Needing desperately to speak, but unable to speak, she tears up the pillows on her bed and fills the room with a snowstorm of feathers. The effect is like a silent assault upon the spectator; the soft violence of it expresses the agony of a mental and physical condition identifiable with the common frustrations of everyday life.

The silence intensifies it. Accustomed as we are to sound in the cinema, and often to sound that is very loud, silence and small noises have the benefit of contrast. A wheeze in the dark gains added menace, as in the Blake Edwards thriller *Experiment in Terror* (1962; re-titled *Grip of Fear* in the U.K.), where the sunny locale of a San Francisco suburb is converted abruptly into darkness and isolation when the heroine (Lee Remick) drives into her garage and the door closes. Out of the confining darkness comes an asthmatic wheeze. The girl is seized from behind, a hand is placed over her mouth, and a wheezing voice threatens her. The expert suspense culminates in the death of the wheezer at a crowded baseball park where he had hoped to avoid detection in the throng. Precious little compassion was afforded the criminal, who was not only afflicted with asthma but also mad, two misfortunes that were seemingly employed to make him all the nastier. Whereas a monster of science fiction will at least earn a morsel of pity, this human monster went unmourned, except perhaps by the mother of a crippled child whose medical bill the criminal had paid.

Compassion for criminals who are mentally ill need not obliterate sympathy for their victims. Sometimes a victim is driven mad by sane rogues. Decaying Charlotte (Bette Davis) in Robert Aldrich's *Hush, Hush, Sweet Charlotte* (1964), is put upon in this way. Her crumbling Louisiana mansion offers noises in the night. Small noises: a distant piano, the echo of a song, uncanny reminders of the lover she thought she killed years ago with a meat axe. She didn't. If we have listened attentively to the dialogue of an earlier scene between Olivia de Havilland and Mary Astor, we know who did. Probably we have guessed, as well, just who is going to so much trouble to drive Charlotte right out of her mind. The suspense is unabashedly antiquated. Traditionally, frightened Charlotte embarks upon a solitary investigation of the small sounds. Lightning illuminates the music room intermittently as Charlotte comes downstairs, lured by the ghostly song. Suspense builds into shock as she beholds a meat axe embedded in the floorboards, a severed hand near by, and (the touch too much, almost begging for reactionary guffaws) the dead man's head in facsimile rolling down the stairs.

Between the suspense build-ups, *Hush, Hush, Sweet Charlotte* is slow. It has been said that the main reason for films being slower in the sixties than they were in the thirties and forties is that the spectator has grown more aware of psychology and wants more exploration of character and motivation. Hitchcock put it rather nicely in the mid-fifties: "In the old days, villains had black moustaches and kicked the dog. They were more simple. The audiences are smarter today. They don't want their villain to be thrown at them with the old-fashioned green limelight on his face. They want to see an ordinary human being with failings."* The same holds true of heroes and heroines. The trick, in a thriller, is to gain this depth without relinquishing an appropriate pace, which will vary according to the specific story but generally needs to be faster than life. For, as Hitchcock has been saying for years, "drama is life with the dull bits cut out".* Melodrama, more so. To cut out the dull bits is not to relinquish contact with life, but rather to emphasise life's problems.

33

It is not unusual, of course, to introduce a passage of suspense into a film that otherwise has nothing in common with thrillers. An extremely suspenseful development is made, very slowly as befits the occasion, in the final phases of Federico Fellini's *Le notti di Cabiria* (1957). Indeed, this could be taken as a prime example of slowly mounting suspense, but it has the advantage of belonging in the context of lyrical realism which has claimed our attention and concern long before the suspense begins.

The simple, trusting Cabiria (Giulietta Masina) is a prostitute and a dreamer, sustaining herself in a hard world with hope of a romantic future. There is an affirmative sign at the end of her vicissitudes, not replacing them but lightening their weight: a serenade from passing youths, responding instinctively to something warm and true in Cabiria's nature. Equivalent optimism was to be expressed in subsequent Fellini films: the girl on the beach at the end of *La dolce vita* (1959), opposing with her purity the corruption symbolised by the landed sea-monster, and, more subtly, in the closing scene of *Giulietta degli spiriti* (1964), the gentle spirit-voices in the sunlight, bringing their solace and peace. Always, before arriving at these affirmative conclusions, Fellini shows life as an oppression to be resisted in order to live. For Cabiria, the weight is greatest in the cliff-top scene with Oscar (François Périer), prefigured at the beginning of the film by an episode presented in the vein of slapstick. This parallel between the ludicrous and the tragic contributes to the tension as well as to the human observation of the cliff-top scene.

At the beginning a man Cabiria loved, and thought of as the fulfilment of her hopes, pushed her into the Tiber and ran off with her purse. Living in dreams, she continues her search and eventually she meets the mild accountant, Oscar. She believes that he loves her, and, as doubt sets in for the spectator but not for her, she gives him her savings. With doubt hovering, we watch them walk slowly through a wood, increasingly enclosed and remote among the trees. Suddenly it is quite clear to us, but still not to Cabiria, that Oscar means to kill her. They reach the edge of a cliff. A good distance below there is water. And now, gazing into his face, Cabiria

...unch ... near the
...tal wood"—Mario
...avid and Clothilde
...ano in LES BONNES
...EMMES.

knows. Oscar does not push her over, but his evident intention is enough to make her wish that he had. The gathering dusk, the greyness through the woods, darken the mood poetically. It is a time suspended between the romantic aspirations of Cabiria and the shadows of reality. On the cliff-top, romanticism is a dim illusion; the peace of the setting is a threat.

Indecision on the brink of murder, again on a cliff-top, is one of several suspenseful occasions in Marco Bellocchio's remarkable film *I pugni in tasca* (1965), a quiet appraisal of a series of melodramatic incidents which arise from the central figure's erratic state of mind. Alessandro (Lou Castel) is an epileptic, driven insane by an energy that can find no clear fulfilment. He becomes obsessed with the idea that to kill the other epileptic members of the family, and then commit suicide, would be an act of altruism. The lack of decision that plagues all his endeavours is at once an added source of suspense and an extension of yet another common weakness. His mother is blind, so it is easy for him to lead her to the cliff and persuade her to go on walking in the same direction, but, having started, he changes his mind and draws her back again, continuing in this confused manner, prolonging the agony. This, and other incidents in the film, could serve equally for a black comedy; but such is the control of Bellocchio's direction that the suspense is integral to the theme of unrest as illustrated in heightened form by the family of epileptics. Alessandro's insanity, provoked by an illness, cannot be dismissed as readily as that of the old-time maniac killer of melodrama. His mental condition does not remove him from the world of the sane and self-satisfied. Criminal is not the word to be applied to him, for his inability to know the difference between right and wrong, and to carry out a preconceived plan of action, is seen as in a mirror that reflects and magnifies but never distorts. There is no poetry, no visual mood, for the terrible scene on the cliff-top. It is daylight and the sun is hard and clear.

Cliff-tops, and woods as well, are apt locations for suspense. The romantic atmosphere becomes readily ironic. Woods offer convenient solitude to lovers and killers alike, and when the lover proves to be a killer, as he often does in the cinema, a wood suits him well. Claude Chabrol drew the utmost romantic irony from a wood in *Les Bonnes Femmes* (1960). Early in the film, a young shopgirl, Jacqueline (Clothilde Joano), becomes aware that a man is following her. He turns up, as if by chance, at places where she happens to be in her free time. He is the muscular type, and Jacqueline is flattered by his evident interest but too shy to offer any sign of encouragement. This man (Mario David) augments his aura of virility by riding a motor cycle and by diving spectacularly into a swimming pool to rescue Jacqueline from the unwelcome attentions of some young pranksters. By this means he makes her acquaintance at last. She agrees to have lunch with him the following Sunday at a modest restaurant near the fatal wood. Things proceed romantically enough, but the spectator has been prepared for suspense during an

earlier scene at a zoo, where the man watched Jacqueline from a distance while Chabrol alternated close-ups of the man's face with shots of a tiger and a gliding reptile which implied not only virility but also menace. Their walk in the wood after the meal is a sensuous one, the silence broken only by the distant cries of birds. They lie on the ground, Jacqueline succumbing to wishful romanticism as his fingers stroke her throat. He strangles her.

While little more than a cipher, this man serves to reinforce the point of the film, an essay in anti-romanticism and, in this episode, a reminder that face values can be deceptive (a recurrent theme in the films of Chabrol). Very suspenseful and succinct, the episode is a highly individual exercise on classic lines.

Of course, in situations of this nature, it is usually a woman who is put upon, and a man who is the aggressor. Occasionally with chilling effect, the situation is reversed. A young man, physically disabled, is the victim of a woman in John M. Stahl's *Leave Her To Heaven* (1945), in a single incident more powerful in itself than the remainder of the work, which is psychological melodrama at its glossiest and well below par for the Hollywood forties. The villainess, Ellen (Gene Tierney), is abnormally possessive. She resents the amount of attention her husband pays to his younger brother, Danny (Darryl Hickman), who is a cripple. One day Danny attempts a little therapeutic swimming in a lake. Ellen is close by him, in a rowing boat, ostensibly to pick him up when he grows tired. Instead, she remains perfectly still in the boat while Danny drowns.

Considered apart from its context, the scene makes an interesting contrast to William Wyler's memorable handling of the passage in *The Little Foxes* (1941) in which Regina (Bette Davis) commits a murder by default, making no move to bring the medicine that will prevent her husband from dying. Elegant and chill, she remains seated in the foregound of the frame, while he moves with great difficulty toward the stairs in the distance. As Ralph Stephenson and J. R. Debrix put it in their book *The Cinema As Art*, the composition stresses "her strong indifference, as if neither the camera nor the heroine even 'turned their head' ". The avaricious woman, isolating herself in her resolve, was photographed in black and white, whereas the wicked Ellen of *Leave Her to Heaven* let her crippled brother-in-law drown amid colourful surroundings. Far from the traditional advantages of misty moor, brooding house, shadowy woods or high cliff, Stahl achieved his suspense against-the-grain in a fashion much favoured by Hitchcock. The sunlit lake was placid, an environment for relaxation that was used instead for swiftly mounting fear. The isolated spot, a picture of serenity, was fraught with danger.

4. Irony

THAT ironic notion of the pleasant place imbued with unexpected menace is far from unrealistic and is capable of many variations. Trains, for example, have any amount of

tension value to be applied ironically against their valid escapist image. Certainly a train which carries us into unfamiliar territory, especially at the start of a holiday and preferably in conditions of extravagant *luxe*, will induce a lightness of heart akin to Jeanette MacDonald's in *Monte Carlo* (1930). "Goodbye to things that bore me," she sings at her train window, confident that romance is waiting "beyond" what she describes as "the blyou horizon". The director, Ernst Lubitsch, epitomises her mood with a shot of the train wheels speeding ever onward and adding their rhythm to the orchestration. Yet trains in films of the thirties are more frequently bound for danger. At the climax of Hitchcock's *Number Seventeen* (1932), a train is tearing through the English country night toward a channel port where it is to be loaded on to the ferry. At the same time, on a road that runs parallel with the railway lines, a bus is trying recklessly to race the train. In the bus, a villain has the driver at gunpoint and the passengers are in a state of advanced hysteria. Certainly they are in no condition to notice the wind-ravaged roadsign to which Hitchcock cuts merrily: "Stop here for dainty teas." The train, meantime, races on ever faster and doesn't even stop, as it should, when it reaches the ferry. It hurtles aboard wildly with a splintering and smashing so jubilant in concept as to disarm intolerance of the obvious model shots.

The same year in Hollywood, Josef von Sternberg had a train-sized train in a jam-packed set to depict the departure of the *Shanghai Express* from old Peiping. Its initial progress is impeded delightfully by a calf taking lunch from its mother smack in the middle of the track in front of the engine. Languidly resting by a corridor window during this delay is feather-hatted Shanghai Lily (Marlene Dietrich), observed with surprise by the occupant of the adjacent window, pith-helmeted Captain Harvey (Clive Brook). Years have elapsed since they met before and fell in love. Much has happened since. "It took more than one man to change my name to Shanghai Lily," she informs him, measuring the words. Uncommonly for its period, *Shanghai Express* is a slow film, dwelling on Sternberg's famous light-and-shadow play, hoarding its suspense, but maintaining its high curiosity value over the years. Subsidiary characters on the train have every bit as much quaintness as their British film counterparts. A cranky old lady, illegally transporting a dog in a basket, tells Shanghai Lily that she keeps a boarding house. "What kind of a house?" "A *boarding* house." "Oh." Even the serious lines are like that, too. In the thick of crisis, Captain Harvey loses a watch that was given to him in happier days by Shanghai Lily. When he tells her it is gone "together with a few ideals", she says that when they reach Shanghai she will buy him another. "Don't bother," he replies; "I'm rather glad I lost it." And eventually, when she keeps her promise, his romantic agony finds expression in the words: "What good is a watch without you?"

As against these blights, accentuated by the passage of time, the visuals have a certain splendour: the remarkably spacious dining car, from which passengers are hauled when revolutionaries stop the train; the celebrated close-up of Shanghai Lily's hands clasped in prayer, gleaming white against the darkness, and the dissolve to smoke from the funnel of the train engine that brings the answer to her prayer;

and, to a lesser extent, the curiously short scene where Hui Fei (Anna May Wong) kills the rebel leader Chang (Warner Oland) in a room that permits of shadowplay with mosquito netting, although a glint of light on the knife blade would have helped to increase the somewhat elusive tension.

The cinema is full of satisfactory samples of the suspense that can be conjured from trains (*Rome Express*, *The Ghost Train*, *The Lady Vanishes*, *Compartiment Tueurs*, and, bluntly, *The Train* are among the familiar titles), but a relatively neglected potential is the yacht, so redolent of luxury and escape, so small against the surrounding water. A fine passage of yacht-suspense is to be found in René Clément's brilliant psychological thriller *Plein Soleil* (1959), with its shadowy doings in bright sunlight. Taken from Patricia Highsmith's splendid novel *The Talented Mr. Ripley*, it includes a murder in a yacht. Tom Ripley (Alain Delon), underprivileged and a bit waspish but charming when it suits him, kills his wealthy chum (Maurice Ronet) and sets about parcelling the body in canvas. The business is clumsy, because the movement of the yacht works against neatness, and getting the parcel overboard is difficult, too; Ripley falls into the water with it.

"Shadows of reality"-
Giulietta Masina and
François Perier in
LE NOTTI DI
CABIRIA.

Afterwards, he assumes the dead man's identity, as both a practical measure and a wish-fulfilment. Aided by his gift for mimicking voices and forging signatures, he carries off the impersonation for a time but remains constantly in danger. Throughout the film, and especially aboard the yacht, the colour camerawork by Henri Decaë is eloquent in sunlight, and strong in moody blues, and it would be hard to think of a film that derives more irony from the contrast between environment and events.

The symbolic value of such an environment is more delicately employed, however, in Roman Polanski's *Noz w wodzie* (*Knife in the Water*, 1961), where the action is confined to a yacht for the greater part of the film's length. The tensions are both psychological and social, related specifically to communist Poland and yet basically identifiable with western attitudes as well. There are three characters: Andrzej (Leon Niemczyk), his wife Christine (Jolanta Umecka), and a young student (Zygmunt Malanowicz) to whom they have extended their equivocal hospitality. At first they have given him a lift as far as the water in their car, and then the husband has invited him to share their yachting weekend. Andrzej looks upon his yacht as a token of the status he has earned. In middle-age he clings to status, nervously. Instinctively he resents the student, who is manifestly virile and non-conformist. Moreover, Christine, blandly enough, is lolling about the yacht displaying much flesh, and, one way and another, Andrzej feels challenged to assert his superiority. Knowledgeable about sailing, he attempts to humiliate the student by a show of efficiency, but the younger man has his own accomplishments. In a test of stamina, Andrzej flattens his hand, palm down, while the student expertly and swiftly dance-jabs the point of a knife between the extended fingers. Sexually ambiguous, highly sophisticated, the suspense is continually underlined by environment. The yacht and its accoutrements are the tangible consolations of Andrzej, bolstering his confidence, and yet the student has but to lie on deck, basking in the sun, against the freedom symbols of sails and water, to look completely at one with his surroundings, as if by right of his youth and strength he had virtually taken possession.

A degree more obvious than yachts, when it comes to irony, are islands. Drenched by arc lamps, the sarong-wrapped Dolores Del Rio and Joel McCrea could bask romantically, in *Bird of Paradise* (1932), in a Hollywood idyll to be perpetuated later in the same decade (and into the next) by Dorothy Lamour and assorted stalwarts, with merely the trad crocodile or volcano to disrupt, in the name of action, the bland escapist mood. While it would be unseemly to overlook the poetic-actuality cinema of islands already explored by Flaherty, and indeed Murnau, the fact remains that a glossy aura is the dominant memory, ripe to be debunked.

In one of Polanski's British-made films, *Cul-de-Sac* (1966), a middle-aged misfit (Donald Pleasence) cuts himself off from the hostility of the world by living in an old castle ("my fortress") on an island off the coast of Northumberland. Yet the outside world intrudes, with black-comedy suspense, and the desolate location constantly gives the lie to the misfit's notion of an idyllic retreat.

Primitive but notable precedents to this kind of irony were already manifest in the early Hollywood thirties, while the glamour-sarongs and palm trees and tropic moons maintained the norm. Count Zaroff (Leslie Banks) in *The Most Dangerous Game* (1932, directed by Ernest Schoedsack and Irving Pichel; U.K. title, *The Hounds of Zaroff*) and Dr. Moreau (Charles Laughton) in *The Island of Lost Souls* (also 1932, directed by Erle C. Kenton) are both misfits in normal society who have taken up residence on remote islands in order to do things that would not be tolerated in civilised communities. Aware of their moral, as well as territorial, remove from the rest of the world, they are lethally disposed toward outsiders who encroach, through force of circumstance, upon their domains.

Count Zaroff goes to some pains to create such circumstances, because he needs the outsiders. By shifting the lights that give warning of a dangerous reef, he causes shipwrecks. This alone would be sufficient to put him on the base level of Sir Ralph the Rover, who "cut the Bell from the Inchcape Float". His motivation, though, is nothing so elementary as black-hearted spite. Zaroff, cold and cultured, is a hunter, dedicated to the chase. He is driven, no doubt, by much the same sense of challenge as drives more moderate adventurers to cross rough seas on a raft or to climb the most treacherous of mountains. Only, in Zaroff's case, he doesn't do it because "it's there" (indeed he has to put it there). He does it, really, because he's bored. Sated with experience, having proved his mastery over the limited intellects of animals, he provides himself with prey of an intelligence nearer to his own.

As the film begins, two freshly shipwrecked prospects arrive at his island mansion. They are sturdy Bob Whitney (Joel McCrea) and beautiful Eve Trowbridge (Fay Wray). Zaroff greets them hospitably, wines and dines them nobly, and then gives them a nasty hint of his predilection in a superb *frisson* line: "Here on my island, I hunt the most dangerous game."

At dawn, Bob and Eve are given a head start in the surrounding jungle, before Zaroff with bow and arrow, hounds and henchmen, tracks them down like wild beasts.

The valid, if simplified, psychology which informs the melodramatic figure of Zaroff, and the swiftly increasing apprehension of his guests (the film runs little more than an hour) give the preliminaries a keen tension, although, seeing it in retrospect, allowances have to be made for the theatricality of the period. Rudimentary to the point of absurdity is an after dinner scene when Zaroff plays the piano while Bob and Eve whisper furtively in a window seat about the dreadful realisation that has dawned on them. When the piano recital is over, Eve nudges Bob and says "Applaud." It is subject, rather than sense of cinema, that holds.

Filmic values are stronger in *The Island of Lost Souls*: indeed, markedly so, when one keeps in mind that the two films belong to the same year. But Dr. Moreau is more way-out, and therefore less disturbing, than Zaroff. Scientifically, in his island laboratory, Moreau gives savage animals the characteristics of human beings, with varied results. The story is derived from H. G. Wells, and the god-manqué doings of Moreau caused the film to be banned in the U.K. for twenty-seven years.

Moreau does not welcome visitors, but he gets one anyway. Edward Parker (Richard Arlen) is another sturdy shipwreck survivor; and his fiancée, Ruth Walker (Leila Hyams), shows up on the island as well, looking for him. Their lives are in peril now, because Moreau doesn't want any hint of his activities to be carried back to the outside world. Before Ruth gets there, Parker is afforded some exotic sex-relief in the person of Lota the Panther Woman (Kathleen Burke), who is the most physically successful of Moreau's experiments. Lota, in her dumb-vamp way, stirs Parker to compassionate embraces, but he gets a nasty jolt when her fingernails turn into talons as they penetrate his shoulder muscle. More articulate than Lota, but exceedingly hairy, is the Sayer of the Law (Bela Lugosi), who would appear to be a transmogrified ape. Moreau has assigned to him the task of indoctrinating the anthropoid populace with certain regulations, all designed to glorify and safeguard Moreau himself. Laughton's Moreau is neatly plump, fastidiously dapper, with a small black moustache and nifty little beard, speaking with a supercilious refinement that can give place impulsively to a neurotic shout. It is the shout we hear first, when he is alarmed at the prospect of having to harbour a stranger, and it returns at full strength for the climax when the converted animals, led by the Sayer of the Law, bear down rebelliously upon their whip-wielding creator. Hero and heroine, like the pair in Zaroff's clutches, escape at the end in a little boat. A back-projected volcano is erupting on the island behind them, just to make sure that all the necessary eliminations are made.

Again there is no gainsaying that the absurdities of the period break through. The dialogue is especially quaint. The hero, at his first sight of an animal-man, whose hair is long and leonine and whose flabby lips barely cover his fangs, inquires in mild perplexity, "Who's that guy?" When the heroine is transported to the island by a helpful sailor, a primeval face ogles her through some bushes, whereupon she emits a full-throated scream, but regains her poise on the instant and turns to the sailor with a reassuring "Pay no attention to me." On the other (more consequential) hand, the atmosphere is quite cunningly established by way of mysterious sea-mist to start with, followed up by exotic

45

*"The prey"—
Dorothy McGuire
in THE SPIRAL
STAIRCASE.*

island vegetation. The camera roves smoothly past large and glossy leaves, leading us in eerie exploration. The studio look is there, but it is aptly strange. A certain amount of exterior shooting was done around Catalina Island; according to Elsa Lanchester's book *Charles Laughton and I* the going was pretty arduous when actors and animals were taken over in the same boat: "The sea was rough and the animals were nearly all sick ... the stench [became] overpowering. The actors threw their lunch-boxes overboard ... Charles made the return trip by seaplane."

5. Phobia

INSTINCTIVE dread is frequently evoked in the cinema; and while those who watch from the extremities of cool cynicism or sheer bone-headedness might well remain unmoved, for the rest the experience is with any luck cathartic. A representation of claustrophobia works by rule of contrast in the film medium, which has accustomed us to open spaces and freedom of action. To deprive us of these things, suddenly, is to gain the emotional advantage: an instant brainwash, as it were. Again, isolation is of the essence and the setting is vital. Cellars and sewers are apt. So are mirrored walls, with their heartless illusion of depth and space, and their taunting multiple reflections of the person confined within them.

To a cellar, Freddie Clegg (Terence Stamp) brings his anaesthetised prey (Samantha Eggar) in William Wyler's *The Collector* (1965), with the intention of keeping her isolated there until she learns to love him. In the sewers beneath Vienna, Harry Lime (Orson Welles) tries unsuccessfully to elude his pursuers in Carol Reed's *The Third Man* (1949). And the mirror maze, at a San Francisco fairground, encases the wicked Elsa Bannister (Rita Hayworth) as bullets shatter her many glamorous reflections and end her life in *The Lady from Shanghai* (Orson Welles, 1947). A claustrophobic trial of strength for James Bond (Sean Connery) in *Dr. No* (Terence Young, 1962) involves terrible intensities of heat and cold as he squirms and drops through horizontal and vertical cylinders. The soundtrack is increasing the tension, too, on such occasions, with echoes of footsteps in the Vienna sewers or a sudden metallic slithering noise as Bond loses his footing.

Yet, before sound had happened to the cinema, the images

themselves were enough for the purposes of claustrophobic suspense. Indeed, sounds apart, all of the elements I have cited were present in one venerable film of the silent days, Rupert Julian's *The Phantom of the Opera* (1925).

"I have brought you five cellars deep . . . because I love you," say the dialogue captions on behalf of the Phantom (Lon Chaney), as he tries to reconcile a startled young soprano to the isolation in which he plans to woo her. The Phantom, painfully aware of his unlovable ugliness and emphatically mad but not without pathos, is a far and simplified cry from Freddie Clegg, whose inferiority complex has been caused by the social and educational gap that yawns between him and the girl he has collected. Basic currency has remained valid, however. Freddie has prepared his cellar with creature comforts and luxury items for the girl. The Phantom has furnished a boudoir with seductive drapes and a boat-shaped bed. For actually sleeping, as distinct from the escape-drifting he has so diffidently in mind, the Phantom prefers a coffin. The touching attempts to make cellars tolerable, and perhaps even agreeable, serve merely to increase the suspense, because the effect these places have on the incarcerated girls is the opposite of what their captors intended. The furnishings, testifying to deep forethought, make it clear that tenancy is meant to be fairly long-term. At the same time, such pathetic evidence of the desire to charm, and of a species of love least likely to be requited, inclines the spectator to grant the psychopath a share of the sympathy that is going mainly to the girl.

The Phantom's cellar is approached by a subterranean waterway, which looks romantic but is formed, as a caption tells us, of "seepage from the Seine". Thus we have a cellar surrounded by a sewer. Not only that, but a mirrored room as well, to which two men who try to rescue the soprano are quickly confined, and then subjected, by means of one of the Phantom's scientific devices, to intense heat. Gasping for breath, tearing at their collars, tormented by their repetitive reflections in the mirrored walls, they are not to be spared the cold treatment either. Water comes flooding in, presumably from the sewer, and steadily it fills the room until the heads of the two prisoners are touching the ceiling as they struggle for breathing space.

Claustrophobia in *The Phantom of the Opera* is suggested the more strongly by contrast with the spacious settings elsewhere in the film, representing parts of Paris and the sumptuous opera house. In the early scenes of apprehension, when stage hands shudder and the girls of the *corps de ballet* trip a staircase to safety in agitated unison, the looming shadow of the Phantom extends across a stony wall. The image endures across the years. Seen again at this remove in time, the film's crude technique and static theatricality prohibit involvement. Yet the occasional image, and very many details in the concept of suspense, hold a lasting fascination.

One notable example occurs when the two new managers of the Opéra, who have laughed off rumours that the place is haunted, venture into the mysterious Box 5. First, in the corridor outside the box, they encounter a formidable *ouvreuse*, who advises them not to go in because the box has been taken already by its usual occupant, a man whose face she has never seen (the Phantom wears a sort of veil) and whose voice she has heard only once: we gather that once was enough, even for her. Nevertheless, with some pomposity, the managers do go in. The box is evidently fairly large. They stand well back and look startled. Then there is a

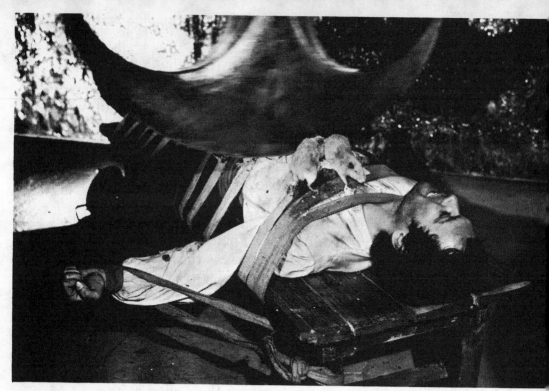

"A dark subterranean room"—Maurice Ronet in LE PUITS ET LE PENDULE.

cut to the sight they behold: the back of the phantom, who is seated close to the edge of the box, concentrating on the performance. Another cut shows us the extravagant terror on the faces of the managers before they hurry out.

The build-up with the *ouvreuse* and then the darkness inside the box serve as warnings that something pretty strong is to come, and sure enough it does: our first substantial sight of the Phantom, who until this point has been glimpsed fleetingly as a shadow. Even now, we are not shown his face. Suspense continues in respect of his appearance, let alone the deeds he might perpetrate.

Silent acting being what it was (with distinguished exceptions), I find it impossible to be sure whether or not the terror of the managers before they leave the box was meant in its day to ease the nervous strain with a little comic relief. It seems quite probable, however, that this was the intention behind the hilarious behaviour of the star soprano. On two occasions, this unhappy woman confronts the management with notes she has received from the Phantom, decreeing disaster if she sings her usual role of Marguerite on certain

*"Animal resources"—
Robert Ryan in
INFERNO.*

nights. *Faust*, most aptly, is the Phantom's favourite opera. He envisages the young soprano as Marguerite; and the girl, for her own part, is delighted to replace the star and make her name (little dreaming of the price she will be required to pay, five cellars deep). The star soprano, while disturbed by the Phantom's messages, is at the same time profoundly indignant. She makes plain her wrath to the management in a flow of language accompanied by operative gestures, arms semaphoring her meaning and requiring no help from dialogue captions. While the young soprano, when under pressure, goes in for facial exercises of a similar order, her gestures are considerably less athletic, and therein lies our clue, perhaps, to what is intended to be funny and what is not.

Dead serious and alarmed, the girl, now afforded the star dressing room, but with her triumph diminished by intimations that the Phantom is after her, opens wide her eyes in fear as the handle of the dressing room door makes the classic slow turn. (The door opens to reveal the anti-climactic hero, who isn't much help and in no way undermines the suspense.)

The eyes of Lon Chaney as the Phantom suggest that he treated this as a thinking role. The face, when not masked, is so grotesquely distorted that externalised acting would have done well enough, but one can guess that Chaney was not prepared to settle for that. It is on his account, as much as anybody's, that the presence of the Phantom dominates the film. In fact the visual compositions are mostly blunt, except for the shadowplay, the ironic-romantic views of the underground waterway, and one histrionic pose of the Phantom on top of the opera house, his cloak billowing in

51

the night, a creature both menacing and pathetic as he overhears a conversation between heroine and hero. If these
compositions are exceptions, there is an extra visual bonus
throughout the film: a tinted print. Apparently the tinted
version is rare. The National Film Theatre in London ob-
tained a print from the Canadian Archive, and I was aston-
ished by the power of it. Although I had seen the occasional
silent film, and even an early talkie or two, in which certain
sequences were tinted for mood, I have never known a case
where the use of tinted monochrome increased the impact so
strongly. For the early part of the story, a sepia tint heightens
the grandeur of the opera house and deepens with the sub-
dued lighting backstage to intensify the shadow on the wall.
After quite a long time with sepia, abruptly the screen turns
red. A caption, backed by a drawing of the Phantom in
silhouette, informs us that something is untoward in the
ceiling of the opera house, where a large chandelier hangs
suspended above the audience. The famous sequence of the
falling chandelier (the means whereby the Phantom makes
good his threat when the star soprano is performing despite his ominous letter) is crude in execution. A shot
looking up toward the chandelier, from the viewpoint of
those immediately below it in the audience, holds the
necessary sense of danger, but the subsequent shot of the
cumbersome thing lying inelegantly across several rows of
stalls, as well-heeled Parisians run in panic all around it, is
minimised by the comforting but improbable circumstance
that nobody seems to have been hit. On the other hand, the
redness, virtually hitting us between the eyes, adds an impact
that the image itself rather lacks. Later, red is used again
for the celebrated set-piece where the Phantom, in a skull-
like mask, arrives at the *bal masqué* by way of the grand staircase. The grouping of the crowd, shrinking back to give him
plenty of room, is no more than a perfunctory bit of stage
management, and the camera angles are unremarkable, but
again this adjunct to the *mise en scène*, this flooding of the
screen with red, commands the eye. For the subterranean and
cellar scenes, the tinting is watery blue and pale greenish-
yellow, which might have worn paler with time but, even so,
the sinister-romantic atmosphere is well served. All of which

goes a long way toward giving the lie to that persistent notion that colour is never so conducive to suspense as black-and-white.

A film of 1956 that harked back to the idea of tinted monochrome was *La traversée de Paris*, a bitter comedy directed by Claude Autant-Lara. Set in Nazi-occupied Paris, the story concerns the events of a single night. Two Frenchmen walk through the unfrequented streets of the city, with suitcases full of black-market pork. (The film was shown in the U.K. in black-and-white, under the title of *Pig Across Paris*.) The men are in peril from the Nazis, who are apt to be alerted by hungry dogs that smell the pork and give chase. Simultaneously, there is rigorous social comment. French attitudes are depicted as selfish, hardened by the conditions of occupation. Ironic contrast is drawn between the two men who share the dangerous mission. One of them (Jean Gabin) is a well-to-do painter, indulging in what he regards as an enlivening adventure, while the other (Bourvil) is very poor and relies upon such excursions to earn his living. After many a nervy escape, they are captured. The painter is released, on

account of his privileged status in life and art, while the humbler man is taken away to prison camp.

In the tinted version, the greater part of the film is blue, deepening in the dark streets (or the studio reconstructions of streets), with a sky devoid of stars. The sky, the danger, and the deep blue combine to give a shut-in feeling. The streets are not free. The long walk becomes a claustrophobic experience in a city enclosed and unsafe.

The epilogue is tinted sepia. Ten years have passed, and it is daylight. The painter is about to take a holiday, and at the railway station the porter who carries his bags is the humble black-marketeer with whom he shared a night's work long ago. On their mutual recognition of one another, the film ends. The warmth of the sepia tinting is ironic, a superficial comfort, and in both the "blue mood" and the "sunny" epilogue, the social comment is expressed more strongly than in black-and-white.

A more pronounced case of a dominant warm colour applied ironically to a contrasting situation is the famous Prairie Stop episode in Hitchcock's comedy-thriller *North by Northwest* (1959). Somewhere between Chicago and Indianapolis, Roger O. Thornhill (Cary Grant) gets off a bus to keep an enigmatic appointment. He finds himself isolated, not in a confined space but in the centre of a flat and limitless landscape, with a few cornfields. Here he is murderously attacked by a low-flying plane. Flinging himself to the ground at the first assault, then running fast across the dusty earth with the plane close behind him, then plunging into some tall cornstalks and lying low while the plane douses him with clouds of insecticide, Thornhill's predicament is of

a kind to chill the blood. Against the grain, and with sufficient rationalisation in the fact that it's a hot afternoon,
Hitchcock had the entire sequence shot through a yellow
filter. The effect is a subtle variation on the tinting method.
The entire film is in colour, but for this one episode the
colour is dominantly amber, accentuating the heat of the day
and contrasting it to the cold sweat of the circumstances.

Despite the highly sophisticated comedy of *North by Northwest*, its excitements are nicely judged and this set-piece at
Prairie Stop has the whiff of realism: location shooting,
genuine plane, and so forth. Yet, in conventional terms of
realism, the colour contradicts certain details of what has
gone before and what is to follow. Thornhill's face, far from
turning pale with terror, is endowed by the filter with a tan
several shades deeper than the Cary Grant norm. Throughout
the film he wears the same suit, except for a short time when
he is disguised in the stolen uniform of a railway porter. The
suit is grey, give or take an occasional tinge of blue. At
Prairie Stop, abruptly, it is brown. It stays brown, on account
of the filter, until the following sequence when he arrives
back in Chicago at night with the Prairie Stop dust still on
the suit which has become blue-grey again.

This daring use of colour for mood, defying routine
realism and thereby creating a sequence that *felt* real, has
a certain affinity with the passage in John Huston's *Moby
Dick* (1955) where the ship is becalmed. The entire film blends
colour and monochrome in the final print, giving a patina
appropriate to allegory; and for the stillness of the ship, the
images are suffused in a golden haze. The eyes of the men
are drawn toward the doubloon that Ahab nailed to the
mizzenmast early in the voyage, a promised reward for any
sailor who would find him the white whale. Now, unable to
make progress and fatigued by the extreme heat, these men
are taunted by the gold of the doubloon. The haze is too rich
for indolence. It works relentlessly upon the nerves, suggesting
very palpably the aggravated tension.

Another subjective impression of tension is gained by a
suffusion of red in Buzz Kulik's *Warning Shot* (1966), a
thriller in which the colour is otherwise naturalistic. When the
hero (David Janssen) is beaten up by four younger men who

spring at him suddenly in a small corridor, the picture becomes totally red and at the same time the tempo shifts into slow motion. Against the realistic grain, the brutal attack takes on the look of dance drama. The subjective red shock of the assault is so swift as to destroy the victim's equilibrium. Panic is accelerated, but simultaneously and with disquieting incongruity the slow movements imposed upon the actors give the impression of a bad dream in which suffering is prolonged.

Both Huston and Kulik, in quite different situations, have achieved fairly direct subjective impressions, whereas Hitchcock at Prairie Stop applied the incongruous amber warmth in a manner more oblique. The gold in *Moby Dick* and the red in *Warning Shot* impinge immediately. In each case, it is fitting to the purpose that the spectator should be very conscious of the dominant colour. In *North by Northwest* on the other hand, the dominant amber dissolves in with a magnificently composed long-shot of great space and quietude. The colour is not the first thing one notices. It merges cunningly with the image, so that its contrast to the naturalistic colour that has gone before is not immediately marked. The mood creeps up on us. The suspense in this sequence begins slowly and then accelerates fast. In a sense, on account of the hot afternoon and the flat landscape, the atmosphere is somnolent. Yet, at the same time, we sense a certain unease. The dominant colour implies a strangeness. Roger O. Thornhill, when he gets off the bus and waits, is expecting something a bit rum, but he doesn't know what. Then with the attack by the plane, the drowsy but uneasy atmosphere is endowed with swift suspense. It is one of Hitchcock's finest essays in the unexpected.

Also, the Prairie Stop sequence is one of the cinema's strongest evocations of agoraphobia. A fear of public places and open spaces would not come unbidden, one feels, to a man like Roger O. Thornhill. Indeed, a public place, the crowded railway station where he could be lost in the throng and elude his pursuers, was a boon to him in the sequence immediately preceding the contrasting one in the empty landscape. So, in this ominous vastness, the irrational sensation of agoraphobia is rationally motivated. Yet for Thornhill, as for even the least neurotic of spectators, there is conceivably a submerged defensive instinct that responds to given surroundings at given times with a mental reflex that in more troubled individuals would amount to phobia. It takes no very great stretch of the imagination to understand that open space might give rise to a panic as frightening in its own way as the sensation of being shut in a confined space.

The implicit fear in a long-shot, which might in other circumstances be majestic or escapist, is very pronounced when a camera in a helicopter travels away from a solitary man in a desert, gradually widening our view of the space around him and reducing him to a small and vulnerable speck in the distance. A shot like this concludes the violent thriller *Œil pour œil* (André Cayatte, 1957), in which a doctor (Curt Jurgens) is pursued into the desert by a man (Folco Lulli) who holds him responsible for the death of his wife.

Not dissimilarly, the threat of distance is the mainspring of suspense in Roy Baker's *Inferno* (1953). Every bit as melodramatic as its title implies, it has nevertheless a deeper value as a study in resilience. At the outset our sympathies are not

"Red on the snow"—Claude Giraud in UN ROI SANS DIVERTISSE-MENT.

engaged on behalf of Donald Carson (Robert Ryan), a millionaire who occupies himself in dissipated sprees. Money-making is no problem. He has plenty. Yet he retains the acquisitive urge. So he goes on an expedition into the desert to search for a manganese deposit, in company with his wife Geraldine (Rhonda Fleming) and her lover Joseph Duncan (William Lundigan). All three are less than likeable, disposing the spectator to observe them at first with detachment. Then, when Carson falls from his horse and breaks a leg, and the wife and her lover abandon him to die in the desert, pity is stirred, though still balanced with contempt. Presently this contempt is diminished as pity is merged with admiration. Carson dredges up some will power and a deal of ingenuity. He is on a ledge overlooking a canyon. There is a drop of something like a thousand feet. Contemplating his position he makes a splint out of tent pegs, sets his broken leg, secures a rope to the rocks and makes the long and arduous descent into the canyon. At a certain point, inevitably, the rope slips and he falls the rest of the way. Regaining consciousness, he sustains himself with milk from a cactus. He shoots a rabbit, but a coyote grabs it and makes off. The insolent millionaire, thrown upon his animal resources, is maddened by frustration but strengthened by the instinctive will to survive. A welter of melodramatic action, involving the wife and her lover again, resolves the plot bitterly.

The remarkable suspense passage of Carson alone in the desert owed much to the three-dimension colour process for which it was made. Unluckily it was completed just as the 3D vogue of the early fifties was on the wane, and, in many cinemas, *Inferno* was shown flat. By a stroke of good fortune, I caught a screening in 3D before this decision was made. The process, technically crude despite the fact that spade work had been done years before, had suffered during the vogue from a lack of imagination. The potential was squandered in a welter of funfair trickery, with much emphasis on the prank of throwing things "out of" the screen "into" the audience. Certainly *Inferno* had its rearing rattlesnake and hurtling rocks, but it was the only film of the 3D phase in Hollywood to take proper dramatic advantage of depth in the background. The vastness of the desert, stretching away toward a distant horizon, intensified Carson's isolation to a degree much greater than one might have supposed. As in all 3D work of that period, foreground figures tended to have the look of cardboard cutouts from time to time. Also the perspectives seemed rather stretched, and the black surround of the screen, seen through the required 3D spectacles, became restricting, as if one were looking through a hole. Even so, the background depth of the desert scenes in Baker's film gave me cause to regret that, on the very brink of discovery, the possibilities of the 3D process were thrown away.

It is conceivable, though, that the persistent emphasis on space has led inventive *cinéastes* more than once to the opposite extreme, not merely to make a change but to rise to a challenge, because, given the initial advantage of contrast when the setting is claustrophobic, the director is obliged to sustain interest and avoid visual monotony. Overcoming restrictions can be an engrossing technical exercise in itself, which might be one of the reasons why Edgar Allan Poe's *The Pit and the Pendulum* has attracted several film-makers. The version I favour personally is Alexandre Astruc's: *Le puits et le pendule* (1963).

The screenplay adheres very closely to Poe. During the Spanish inquisition, a prisoner (Maurice Ronet) is condemned to death. He is thrown into a dark subterranean room, where he gropes about and discovers that a deep pit yawns in the centre of the floor. When unseen eyes observe that he hasn't stumbled into it, guards enter the dungeon and place him on a low bed, to which he is tied down, supine, the long surcingle wrapped tight across portions of his body to keep him fairly still. Left alone in this position, looking up toward the ceiling, he beholds a descending pendulum with a crescent blade of steel. By slow degrees it swings down toward his defenceless body, gathering momentum as it comes. The prisoner takes some meat from a bowl near the bed, and smears it across the portion of the surcingle that binds his chest. This attracts rats. They gnaw through his bonds just in time. He knows at once that his escape has been witnessed by his persecutors, because now the pendulum ascends quickly to the ceiling. The escape is temporary. The iron walls of the dungeon begin to radiate an intense heat. At the same time they move toward him, reducing the size of the place, forcing him to the edge of the pit. The tension is relieved abruptly by the arrival of French troops who have taken Toledo. They set the prisoner free.

Astruc's fidelity to Poe is not without its wise amendments. The pendulum's blade, considerably longer than the "foot in length" that Poe specified, has a magnified menace as the camera looks up at it, offering us the subjective view. On the other hand, discretion has been exercised regarding the number of rats. Had they literally "leapt in hundreds" upon the prisoner, there would have been a macabre absurdity to the scene, whereas one or two, nibbling away helpfully and at the same time displaying a dangerous interest in the prisoner's throat, make their keen minority contribution to suspense.

Much of Poe's narrative is preserved as interior monologue, aiding the visuals by affirming the prisoner's state of mind, the dazed condition that hinders him as he strives to think up ways to save his life. Also, without diminishing the suspense, the slow agonising passage of time as the pendulum descends can be conveyed most palpably in economic images accompanied by the words "*Que sert-il de raconter les longues, longues heures . . . il s'écoule des jours.*" Aside from such practicalities, interior monologue in cinema, and especially in this specific instance, has a holding power stronger than dialogue, and indeed stronger than silence. To the voice of Ronet, unnerving sounds are added: the hiss of the pendulum increasing in volume as it gains velocity; the metallic creaking of the walls as they move relentlessly closer. Voice and sounds and images are merged, in a fusion of

. . natural desire
. . cape"—François
. . rier in UN
. . DAMNÉ À MORT
. . T ÉCHAPPÉ.

"*Ambitious entomologist . . . ruthless villagers"—Eiji Okada in WOMAN OF THE DUNES.*

61

elements that become wholly cinematic and indigenous to the experience. At the moment of seeing and hearing, one does not categorise them automatically as separate factors. Occasionally, sparingly, there is music: "*Je priais le ciel, je le fatiguais de mes prières de faire descendre l'acier plus rapidement*" is accompanied by a choir singing baroque religious music of the eighteenth century.

Many of the visuals are subjective. After a quick impression of the trial at the beginning, where the death sentence is pronounced while the prisoner is numbly bemused by candle flames, we are soon with him in the cell. Here Poe decreed "the blackness of eternal night". The prisoner must feel his way about. Short of some invention to approximate "the feelies" that were forecast satirically by Aldous Huxley in his novel *Brave New World* (which the cinema, in one of its funfair moods, has only attempted in a seat-device to impart an electric shock at a moment of crisis), Astruc understandably permits some meagre light to seep into the dungeon. Visually he conveys the prisoner's discovery of the pit, the stumble in semi-darkness now, the sensation of touch converted into visible terms. The "feel" is easy to imagine when the picture is corresponding to the situation as Poe described it: ". . . my chin rested upon the floor of the prison, but my lips, and the upper portion of my head . . . touched nothing."

The film is in black-and-white. It was made initially for television, but I saw it in a cinema and wondered at the time how so much darkness would have fared on the television screen which is usually viewed with some light in the room, converting blackness to a pale grey. As seen in the cinema, the blackness is sufficient to the purpose, and black-and-white photography is apt for the early part of the story. It could be argued, though, that tinting, or colour photography in which a single colour is dominant, would have been more suitable for the next two phases. Poe wrote of the darkness being alleviated at last by "a wild, sulphurous lustre". Later, the heat from the moving walls brought with it "a richer tint of crimson".

The argument in favour of colour does tend to weaken at the point where idealism and practicality meet in one of their headlong clashes. Technically, there are complications to colour. Even after years of colour films it is still possible to hear an art director lamenting that the colour he intended is not the one that actually turns up on the screen. It is also possible to see in one cinema a print of irreproachable clarity, and in another cinema another print of the same film that diminishes the clarity in fuzz. Indeed, within the same print of the same film, a marked variation of colour quality can occur.

Black-and-white is less inclined to vary in such ways; and, along with its technical advantage, it is undeniably strong on contrasting dramatic values as well as the subtle gradations of grey that help so often to modify a mood. Astruc's *Le puits et le pendule* is in itself an argument in favour of black-and-white. The tonal values hold more nuance than those in the print I saw of Roger Corman's full colour version of the same story, which was elaborated to feature length, whereas Astruc has another advantage in his shorter running time. At half an hour, suggesting the disturbingly slow passage of time with effective succinctness, it is possible to concentrate the suspense. That gasp of relief as the prisoner avoids the blade, followed by an increased tension as the walls close in, is as choice an example of screw-turning as I have experienced. The outcome, if brisk and corny, is inevitably sympathetic. Catharsis has been achieved.

An amusing variation on the moving walls, with concomitant claustrophobia, takes place at the climax of Joseph Pevney's *The Strange Door* (1951), a quaint version of Robert Louis Stevenson's short story *The Sire de Maletroit's Door*. The rakish hero (Richard Stapley) and his bride (Sally Forest) are imprisoned by the mad Maletroit (Charles Laughton). The stone walls of their cell move in, threatening to crush them, but the movement is arrested when Maletroit becomes entangled in a millwheel which drives the wall-mechanism. During the respite caused by his discomfiture, the captives are released by an old servant (Boris Karloff). Once they are free the walls begin to move again and a table in the cell is crunched. An interesting primitive example, this, of accentuating the relief after a passage of suspense by giving us an idea of what might have happened had rescue not been nigh.

A unique suspense film about incarceration and the natural desire to escape is Robert Bresson's masterpiece *Un condamné à mort s'est échappé* (1956). The story, based on fact, is of a French lieutenant imprisoned by the Nazis in the Fort de Montluc in 1943. Through details, shown in close-up, Bresson expresses the man's dedicated resolve, establishing a mesmerising but unemotional rapport between prisoner and spectator as the man goes to work with whatever unpromising material comes to hand within his cell; the edge of a spoon is sharpened laboriously until it can cut away sections of the door, wire from the bedsprings is slowly fashioned into hooks, or joined with other material to form makeshift ropes. Eschewing any hint of histrionics, François Leterrier (an "unknown": see Chapter 5) as the prisoner is a justification in himself for Bresson's concept of film acting: "If cinema could have been invented before the theatre . . .

"A walk he owes himself"—Mathias Henrikson in KUNGSLEDEN.

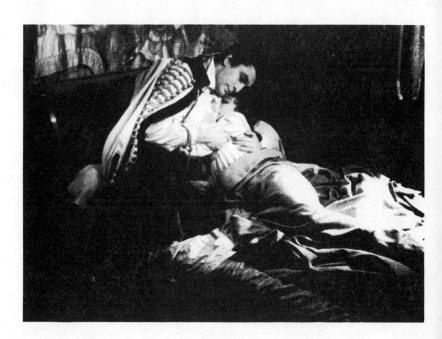

"On one such
visit . . ."—
Jean-Claude Pascal
and Anouk Aimée
in LE RIDEAU
CRAMOISI.

actors, in the present conception, would not exist; the cinema would change its characters for each film, and take them from here and there, from real life."* The perpetual danger that the prisoner will be discovered at his work is intensified when another captive is brought to share the cell. His collaboration in the escape plan will be invaluable, but the lieutenant cannot be sure that this new man is to be trusted. Still with concentration upon detail and situation, rather than any of the customary emotional aids, Bresson tightens suspense more traditionally as the escape is eventually made.

Even closer, and indeed stylised, observation of details (grains of sand, pores of the skin) evokes a cerebral response to Hiroshi Teshigahara's *Suna no onna* (*Woman of the Dunes*, 1963). An ambitious Japanese entomologist (Eiji Okada) is confined by some ruthless villagers to a hut at the bottom of a large hole in the sand, occupied already by a solitary woman (Kyoko Kishida) who is there to shovel away the sand that perpetually menaces the village. Two instinctive dreads, then: claustrophobia within the hole in the sand, agoraphobia in the vastness of sand above. The entomologist is bent upon escape, which is denied him continually. Especially defeating are the steep walls of the hole; down them the sand drifts relentlessly, forbidding a foothold. Suspense runs exceedingly high, but is steadily overcome (to make the point). Gradually the man, not unaided by the therapeutic eroticism of his relationship with the woman, learns to adjust to an isolated and confined existence, and to discover within it an occupation.

He devises a means of distilling fresh water. This in itself becomes so rich a purpose that, forgetting his worldly ambitions, he is content to stay in the hole. When the opportunity to escape is at hand, he does not take it. From the instincts of dread, the film has progressed to an affirmation of human resilience and adaptability.

6. All in the Mind

THE mind of a murderer is often helplessly susceptible to impulses that non-murderers have experienced but have been able to hold in check. For an actor, this knowledge can be useful. Rod Steiger says, "When you play a murderer you have to realise, as all of us have, that sooner or later in our lives we have felt, unfortunately, like killing somebody. The difference is that we had enough rational control not to do it, or went out and had two or three beers to make sure we'd forget about it. The character you're playing usually doesn't do these things because the writer chooses that the murder be committed."*

The thoughtful spectator at a film involving murder is probably gratified, to some extent, by the realisation that he has resisted impulses very similar to those which the murderer on the screen is incapable of resisting. As Martha Wolfenstein and Nathan Leites point out, in their book *Movies: a psychological study*, "the destructive potentialities present in every human being, though in markedly different degrees, find only very partial overt expression".

An elementary identification for the spectator is boredom. A need for release from the routine and the commonplace might be his reason for going to see a film of suspense. In the early 1930s, he would hardly have identified automatically with Count Zaroff's grandiose anti-boredom murders in *The Most Dangerous Game* (see Chapter 3), but thirty years later he might well be given pause by the more delicate and disquieting insanity of the killer in *Un roi sans divertissement* (1963). This murderer's boredom arises from social convention and environment. He is, on the face of it, an ordinary man, a family man. Within him are the seeds of discontent, aggravated by the isolation of the snow-covered village in which he lives. He is not discovered, nor indeed seen, until well toward the end of the film, but we have come to understand his neurotic condition through the wry and sober remarks of an old man, and through the disturbing behaviour of a younger man who has been called in to investigate the crimes.

Un roi sans divertissement, from a novel by Jean Giono, is a fascinating essay in direction by François Leterrier, the former philosophy student who had been chosen by Bresson in 1956 to play the leading part in *Un condamné à mort s'est échappé*, and who decided subsequently to pursue a career in cinema. This was only his second film as director, and it is especially notable for its imaginative and suspenseful use of colour. The snow, thick and silent, covers the nineteenth-century village like a shroud. The remoteness of the place is felt very strongly, the more so because the colour photography comes near, very often, to monochrome. Advantage is taken, sparingly, of obvious contrasts: a spurt of blood that falls upon the snow from the severed neck of a goose, or, at night, the flames of torches against the silent dark.

The inhabitants of the village are alarmed by the disappearances of little girls. Langlois, a young captain of the gendarmerie (Claude Giraud), comes new to the village for the specific purpose of solving the mystery. He talks to a philosophical old man, a retired public prosecutor (Charles Vanel) who lives in the village. They are seated opposite one another across a desk, the camera prowling behind the neck of Langlois as he listens in some amazement to the old man upon whom our attention is focused while the moving camera suggests the unease of Langlois. The opinion being voiced by the old man is that the criminal in the village is probably an ordinary man like any other, as far as appearances go, but that his appetites are richer than average. The ordinariness is something Langlois instinctively repudiates. Handsome and upright himself, he cannot understand how any man could give way to baser instincts. Suspense arises, then, not only from the search for the criminal but also from the young captain's slow recognition of similar base instincts in himself.

It is thought that perhaps a wolf might have carried the children off. So a wolf-hunt is arranged. The old man, seated in a sleigh, wrapped in soft brown furs against the white cold, is an interested but detached observer. With a wry serenity he awaits developments, savouring a pâté of pork fat and juniper that has been offered him by an ex-prostitute, Clara (Colette Renard), who is the landlady of the inn where Langlois is staying. A little group of villagers has gathered by the time the wolf is found and shot, and a voice from among them is heard to remark that now the wolf has been relieved of his boredom. Nobody knows who has spoken. It might have been any one of them. What it serves to make clear is that the wolf is not the culprit, and that the criminal in their midst, making so bold as to speak, is savouring danger. The old man, who has for his part been content to savour the pâté and the psychology, likens the unknown criminal to *"un roi sans divertissement"* who has alleviated his boredom by giving way to blood-lust, a passion thereby equated with "the sport of kings".

Langlois, paying attention to such matters now, and striving to understand the criminal's motivation, finds himself behaving oddly at the inn. In a chilling little scene, we see him holding the body of a small bird he has strangled, lifting the limp creature in pathetic hops across a table, The identification process is not complete. Langlois retains his sense of duty, and prevents himself from assaulting Clara, the innkeeper. But his stability is weakened considerably by the time he discovers the bodies of the missing children, lying in the snow-covered branches of a tree some little distance from the village. In the white stillness, they seem to be sleeping, but they are dead; and immediately after the discovery, Langlois sees a man near by, black-clad against the whiteness. This man, a figure in the middle-distance, not closely seen but unable to conceal himself, begins to walk back toward the village, making no haste and no pretence, virtually leading his pursuer onward across the snow. In a simple but very telling composition, the two men are seen as small black figures in a white landscape. The film is in Franscope, and this shot, with the killer walking at the right extremity of the frame, and the captain at the left extremity following him, is an elegiac variation of the chase theme. Both men move steadily, with snow-heavy steps. The camera, distant, slow-moving, sustains the composition for quite a long time. It holds, suspensefully; and sadly as well. There is a certain bond between the two men, as well as a sense of inevitability in their steady movement.

We are given a shadowy impression of the murderer's home, as Langlois watches him go in and then moves closer to look inside. It is a conventional home, symbolically shadowed. Family words are being exchanged in a conventional way, and then the murderer is left alone for a time and Langlois confronts him, still not entirely identified, still prompted to ask if a man who has a normal home like this can find himself bored. The killer merely replies in the affirmative, quietly, in the manner of one who considers it pointless to elaborate. Langlois takes him out into the snow again, and shoots him.

At the moment of actually killing, Langlois takes on the full identification. Now the film enters its final phase, an extension of the atmosphere that Leterrier has established so subtly. Beyond realism, but on the right side of melodrama, the symbolism of this final phase is superbly judged, a small masterpiece of benighted romanticism. Langlois, a cord stretched tight between his hands, looks through the window of a house in the village. There are children inside. With an effort of will, Langlois turns his passion against himself. In the last frame, the handsome face is dead, and the blood of Langlois is red on the snow.

A more conventionally melodramatic representation of blood-lust is given in the Nicholas Ray thriller *In a Lonely*

Place (1950), which gains much of its strength from Humphrey Bogart's performance as Dixon Steel, a Hollywood writer who so much resents being suspected of a murder he didn't commit that he comes near to actually murdering two people, on different occasions, in mindless rage. The urban environment brings the thing nearer home, perhaps, than the otherworldliness of Leterrier's snow-village, but is necessarily blunt by comparison, thrusting the melodramatic aspect into relief.

A succinct opening scene establishes Steel as a hothead whose creative drive is frustrated by the nature of his work. We see him in his car, which is halted at traffic lights alongside another car. A woman seated beside the driver of this other car recognises Steel as the writer of a movie in which she acted. She remarks on it now, but Steel replies that he makes a point of never seeing the movies he writes. For some reason, the man driving the other car, himself a hothead presumably, takes exception to Steel's words. He claims that Steel is insulting the actress. The two men are ready to get out on to the footpath there and then and have a fight, but the actress protests, the traffic lights change, and the scrap is averted. To this nifty little piece of exposition is added the incidental point that Steel is not the only hothead in town, and we begin to appreciate that his bad temper is an extreme case of the irritability common to many.

A novel that Steel is going to adapt for the cinema has been deposited with a hat check girl, who has taken the opportunity to read it, so Steel invites her home to give him an idea of the plot. She agrees, and recounts the tale with some relish. However, it serves to irritate Steel even more. Later that night, the hat check girl is killed in a car "in a lonely place". The police suspect Steel, but a woman unknown to him, Laurel Gray (Gloria Grahame), who has just moved into an apartment that overlooks his own, is able to give evidence that seems to exonerate him.

Initially, Steel is rather intrigued by the case. A policeman and his wife, both friends of Steel, come to visit him, and he persuades them to reconstruct the crime. The zest in Bogart's eye as he directs proceedings is typical of the quiet power he could assert, the fusion of star personality and interior actor

that made his talent ideal for cinema. Steel urges the policeman and his wife to sit together on a small sofa, like the hat check girl and her killer in a car. The man's left arm is extended forward toward the steering wheel, his right is around the woman's neck. Steel's face takes on a sadistic glee, as the writer's words pour out of him, inciting the policeman to tighten his forearm across the throat of his wife, until, in real fear, she breaks away. In the circumstances, the spectator cannot be sure yet if Steel has really committed the murder of the hat check girl. Bogart's intensity could imply equally that the idea of the murder, and this re-creation of it, is a vicarious satisfaction to Steel. Such is indeed the case. The crime is pinned on quite another person, in an almost off-hand manner, at the end of the film. The concern is primarily with Steel, who is guiltless only by default. He is a character not unlike the men in Antonioni's films, who have settled for mercenary occupations and are consequently frustrated.

An interesting sequence of events begins when Laurel, the girl from the opposite apartment, is called to the police station for further questioning. By now she is seeing Steel quite often, and has fallen in love with him. The police wonder if perhaps they were well acquainted already, when

71

Laurel gave her previous convincing evidence on Steel's behalf. She does her best to persuade them that Steel was a stranger to her then, and she doesn't tell Steel about this further questioning for fear of distracting him from his work, which is going well. Then, one evening, Laurel and Steel join the policeman friend and his wife at the beach. They cook sausages over an open fire. The policeman even ventures to take a swim. Everything, including the back projection, is amiable enough. Then, unintentionally, the policeman's wife lets fall that Laurel has made that second visit to the police station. Steel, instantly resentful at being kept in the dark, leaps to his feet and runs to his car. Laurel runs after him and gets into the car just as he drives off. The car's progress along the coastal road is rapid and dangerous; the tension, slightly blighted by process work that is very evident now, is maintained by well chosen close shots and by Bogart's interior acting which generates thought without words. Laurel offers Steel a lighted cigarette. He refuses in silence, driving recklessly on. A close shot of Laurel's feet, clamping down on her side of the car, applying invisible brakes, is especially helpful. Such details accelerate the suspense to the point where another car, turning into the road, collides with Steel's. Both cars stop. A young man jumps out of the other car, hotly indignant, saying he has just spent money on a paint job. His incensed condition arouses Steel, as did the encounter at the start of the film. This time there are no traffic lights to change and bid him drive on, and Laurel's protests are unheeded. Steel gets out, gives the young man a savage beating, and, having knocked him unconscious, grabs a stone from the side of the road and raises it to bash out his brains. A scream from Laurel arrests the action. Reason returns grudgingly.

When they have driven on for a time, leaving the young man unconscious by the roadside, Steel stops the car and puts his arm around Laurel's neck, forearm close against the throat. Repetition value is tidy here: first the hot blood rising in irritated motorists, and now the return to the demonstrated strangle-hold. Steel's forearm moves instinctively, but does not tighten on Laurel's throat. What might have seemed a fairly trivial *frisson* becomes something more, however,

72

through Bogart's interpretation. Later, when Laurel buys herself a ticket to New York and Steel learns of it, he sets about strangling her, but again the intention is not fulfilled. The urge has strengthened, though, from instinct to intent. The love affair is over.

The story, a tolerable thriller, embodies a simple study of the persecution complex leading to violence. What Bogart made of it is absorbing to watch. Given his face and voice, he might have coasted along quite easily as a rough-diamond star personality. He was one of the personality breed who could appear to dominate, in a medium which by its nature is bound to be dominated by directors. Yet, together with the implicit menace of the character he played in *In A Lonely Place*, there is extreme vulnerability, the feeling of a man in danger, and hardly aware, for all his intelligence, that the danger lies within himself.

Another kind of mental and emotional disquiet, perhaps even more readily appreciated by the average spectator, is that of the man who is placed by circumstances, rather than design, in a position so untenable that he cannot bring

"... a revolver at the back of his neck"— Lino Ventura (centre) in LE DEUXIÈME SOUFFLE.

himself to terms with it. To questions that begin "What would you do if . . . ?" there can be no confident answer, except from those who are so steeped in discipline as to have no true minds of their own any more. Neither murder nor violence is involved in the desperate experience of a man with a dead body on his hands in *Le rideau cramoisi* (1952), the first film directed by Alexandre Astruc. It had been Astruc's intention to film *Le puits et le pendule* at that time, an ambition delayed until a good ten years later (see Chapter 4). Apparently the change was connected with finance, sufficient coming to hand to permit him to engage two leading players instead of just one. The two works have a couple of things in common: both are fairly short, *Le rideau cramoisi* being the longer at three-quarters of an hour, and both employ to admirable effect an interior monologue by the central character instead of dialogue. Also, despite their literary origins, both affirm Astruc's famous wish for a cinema in which "the distinction between writer and director is meaningless". Short of the ideal, which would have writer and director as one creative mind, Astruc's *caméra stylo* made images for *Le rideau cramoisi* that had their own life, in their own medium.

Le rideau cramoisi is from a story written in the nineteenth century by Barbey d'Aurevilly. The words are being spoken in recollection by the central character, thinking back over events that took place several years before but that have remained so strongly in his mind that he virtually relives them as he speaks. Occasionally the words state exactly what the visuals are already showing us, which is not a redundancy but a heightening of impact. More often, the purpose of the words is to express, as in *Le puits et le pendule*, the man's state of mind.

Suspense is created at the beginning, rather over-anxiously, in a flash-forward after the fashion of *The Big Clock* (see Chapter 1) or, for that matter, *Beau Geste*. There are several shots of an officer of the Napoleonic wars riding fast through the deserted streets of a provincial town at dawn. The silence of the hour is broken by the twittering of caged birds as he hurries from a house, and then by the sharpness of his horse's hooves on cobbles. The desperation of his flight is stressed by

one tilted shot, setting the image awry: the device employed
so tellingly by Duvivier for the episode of the epileptic doctor
in *Un carnet de bal*, and parodied so richly when villainy is
afoot in the enlivening *Batman* telecapers of the sixties.

We see the officer departing, and then a curtain billowing
at a window of the house he has left. Beyond the curtain,
through the window, we discern the dead body of a girl. Then
come the credit titles. It is possible that Astruc felt the opening phase of the story to be so leisurely that an initial fillip
would help. He need not have worried. From his iris-in,
spreading a chessboard before us, his images are compelling.
The young officer (Jean-Claude Pascal), billeted in the affluent house of an elderly couple with whom he has no rapport,
lies indolent and bored in his room. His isolation is partly
from choice. As he walks through the provincial streets and
mounts his horse, the interior monologue tells us of his pride
in his resplendent white uniform. He lives "inside it", and
inside himself.

While there are constant hints, not least in the title of the
film, that colour might have been an asset, Astruc's delicate
gradations of black and white, light and shadow, in beautifully composed pictures, give a swift impression of tedium at
the house, before, unexpectedly, his polite mealtime encounters with the elderly couple are strangely brightened by
the return of their daughter from her convent school. The
girl, Albertine (Anouk Aimée), is beautiful but cool in manner. She too, it would seem, keeps herself to herself. But after
a time, the officer comes down to a meal and observes that
the seating arrangement at the table has been changed. Now
Albertine is seated next to him. During the meal, a close shot
beneath the tablecloth shows her hand moving to his thigh,
where it rests for a considerable time. Subsequently she is
cold and withdrawn again. The monologue and the eloquently changing visuals disclose his mounting desire, which
is frustrated for months, until one night, as he lies awake in
his room, his door is opened, creaking in the silence, and
Albertine approaches.

To reach his room at night, Albertine must pass through
the bedroom of her parents, after they have gone to sleep. On
one such visit, when their love making is over, the officer

discovers to his dismay that Albertine is dead. His first thought is to carry the body to its rightful room. He lifts it and goes as far as the stairs, the sweat of fear on his face, but he cannot bring himself to risk the necessary passage through the room of the parents, so he returns to his own room, still with the body. He goes to the window, contemplates throwing her down to the street below, and then realises that it would be apparent that she had fallen from his window. His next thought is suicide. As he takes up his gun and raises it to his temple, the camera pans down diagonally to the body of the girl, coming to rest on a composition that includes the shadow of the officer's leg in the frame and leaves space for his body to fall beside hers. We await the pistol shot, and the falling body. Instead, the pistol falls into the frame. Again he has been unable to complete his intention.

At dawn, the camera outside the window observes the officer's face through the glass and the window frame, more remote than ever, and totally self-centred. Then we see him leave. Swiftly the monologue supplies the missing details, so that it is unnecessary to break the atmosphere with a scene elsewhere. We learn that in the hours before dawn he has told the full story to his superior officer, who has arranged for him to leave the town at once and has promised to talk to the girl's parents. Now the flash-forward is repeated, the fast ride at dawn, the hooves on cobbles, the curtain billowing at the window, and there the film ends.

As an impression of guilt without crime, *Le rideau cramoisi* exists, as Astruc intended, "mid-way between memory and dream". It is an achievement of remarkable subtlety.

Guilt on account of crime is an easier matter to deal with. Poe's *The Tell-Tale Heart*, filmed some half dozen times, lends itself to nightmare imagery. Jules Dassin's version in 1941 was an unusually ambitious short film among the many that the M-G-M studios were turning out at that period. Joseph Schildkraut played the demented murderer who concealed his victim's body under the floorboards, only to be tormented by the imagined beating of the dead man's heart. Dassin took full advantage of the killer's "over-acuteness of the senses", as Poe put it, building tension from the initial observation of the potential victim's blind eye, seen at night

in a shaft of lantern light, obsessively, as if from the murderer's viewpoint. To follow the imagined menace of the eye, the imagined retribution of the heartbeats, increasing in volume as hysteria mounted, accelerated suspense in classic manner.

Fundamentally, it is not so very different, although in detail it is much more intriguing, to be confronted by the guilt-ridden conscience of the man in *Kungsleden* (1965; for the U.K. it became *My Love and I*). The source is a novel by Bosse Gustafsson. As filmed by Gunnar Höglund, it is capable of more than one interpretation, taking so much advantage of the medium's freedom to dart from present to past and to couple memory with imagination, that what we see is virtually taking place within the mind of the central character. He is called Du (You) and is played by Mathias Henrikson. At the age of thirty he is on a solitary hike through the mountains of Lapland, following the track known as the Royal Route. Ten years before, he made the same journey in company with a girl, Leni (Maude Adelson), of whom he is reminded now as he passes through the places they saw together, and as he stays overnight in the wooden huts that stand at intervals along the route. At the beginning his mental flashbacks to their fretful love affair can easily be distinguished from the action that takes place in "the present". Du's hair is combed back from his brow to denote more age, and forward to let us know when he is being ten years younger. When they parted, unhappily, at the end of that earlier journey, Du and Leni had agreed to go their separate ways but to take the Royal Route again a decade later. So Du's present trek is a quest for Leni, a bid to recapture the romanticism that evaporated so quickly, so long ago. And indeed, at each of the huts he sleeps in, he finds Leni's name freshly inscribed in the book that must be signed by those who make use of the facilities. It would seem that she is about a day's walk ahead of him.

Suspense accumulates as Du's recollections disclose a time when Leni struggled with him beside a swift mountain stream. She fell from his grasp into the water and was carried away in the rapid current. Du, young, insecure, angry with her at that moment, made no attempt to go to her rescue. When she emerged eventually, badly shaken by the experience as well as by their previous arguments, the parting took place. And also, the promise to return and try again.

Now, as Du approaches this same mountain stream, the narrative becomes ambiguous. What he sees, or appears to see in "the present", is Leni's dead body in the stream. He hauls the body out of the water, puts it in a sleeping bag, and then runs away. Horrified and exhausted, he arrives by night at another hut, collapses on to one of the bunks and sleeps.

When he wakes in the morning, he sees that one of the other bunks has been occupied by a climber who is already dressed and ready for a vigorous and dangerous ascent. This man, Den Andre (The Other, played by Lars Lind), bears a certain resemblance to Du. Presently Du's imagination pictures again the scene of ten years ago beside the stream, this time in slow motion: the man struggling with Leni is Den Andre,

and the slow motion discloses that he is virtually pushing her into the water. Du persuades himself that Den Andre, in "the present", has murdered Leni. As Den Andre climbs the treacherous mountain, with great skill, Du follows and gets into difficulties. On a small ledge, high up the mountain, he accuses Den Andre of killing Leni. The man, who seems perfectly substantial and rational (although we cannot be sure that he really exists), denies all knowledge of the girl. Du's condition by now is not far from hysteria. Unable to climb higher, unwilling to attempt the precipitous descent, he accepts Den Andre's offer to lower him down the side of the mountain on a strong cord. This operation is begun, but once Du has gained a safe footing he tugs on the cord and Den Andre falls off the mountain. Du regains the ground, and the film ends, leaving us with an intriguing profusion of possible interpretations.

The one I am inclined to favour is that Du's uncouth behaviour toward Leni ten years before has so preyed upon his mind ever since that he believes he has ruined her life and virtually killed her. His journey in "the present" is a gesture prompted by wishfulness and self-reproach. The dead body in the stream is a projection of his imagined guilt. Den Andre is also a figment of his imagination, the substantial image of the confident man of action he would like to have been ten years before. And Den Andre's death is really Du's wishful suicide, which he is not brave enough to carry out in reality.

The fascination, and often the beauty, of Höglund's film resides basically in his clever use of authentic locations, superbly photographed in colour. With a couple of freakish exceptions, the images are what would normally be termed realistic, yet the tormented mind of Du is bending reality more and more. The final sequence on the mountain is extraordinary. No process shooting here. The camera positions might well have been safe, but the height is persuasively dangerous. The only mistake is a close view (probably a studio set-up) of Den Andre falling and screaming, suspended laterally in space. Perhaps this was intended as a deliberate falseness, a clear pointer to the derangement of Du,

"In the wrong place at the wrong time"—
Barbara Stanwyck and Barry Sullivan in JEOPARDY.

but in the circumstances, with Du's imagination at play amid realistic surroundings, the effect jars pretty badly. Also crude is the nightmare Du has in the hut where he sleeps after "discovering the body" and before "meeting Den Andre". This could also be a means of making us realise that Du's mind is awry, but everywhere else in the film there is the more telling implication of dementia amid a natural environment. It seems a pity to go overboard into the obvious, even with the excuse of nightmare; and, since there is any amount of explicit sex, which is rather well done, there was surely no commercial need to include in the nightmare the stamina-test of a bird plucking something long and bloody from the sleeping bag in which Leni's "dead body" had been encased. The nightmare, really, verges clumsily upon expressionism in a film that has no need of it.

Neither Du nor Leni is especially sympathetic. Leni is an unorthodox Jewess, eating pork and sleeping around, a character too proud to bid for compassion from anybody, least of all the spectator. Toughened by history and by life, she survives; but just to let us know, and validly enough, there is a little scene where she watches Laplanders marking the ears of young reindeer, and, transferring our orientation for a moment from Du's mind to Leni's, a monochrome frame or two are cut in, newsreel-raw, showing numbers being branded on forearms in a concentration camp. Leni is no sufferer, however, in her own estimation. With bitterness, and indeed with spite, she reacts. Du, for his part, at the time of their trek ten years ago, is a fumbling puritan. His sex urge embarrasses him no end. He is conscious, too, of a lack of the kind of courage that is so evident in the girl. There is a bridge to be crossed early in the trek, a flimsy looking thing with rapids beneath. Leni frolics across it. Du, reluctant to venture and ashamed on that account, tries to do the same, and slips. Leni comes back and helps him across. His doubts about his manhood are temporarily dispelled the first time he and Leni make love in one of the huts; but the following morning he chides her, puritanically, for bathing naked in a stream and chatting to a passing Laplander at the same time. It is from this point that the possibility of an idyll is blighted

81

by antagonism. Subsequently, provoked by Leni's gibes, he takes her by force, and the guilt-imaginings of murder can be taken to stem from this.

If Leni, while unsympathetic in the conventional terms of cinema, is eminently understandable, so in a more intricate way is Du. Beyond adolescence, he has been mortified in the company of a woman toughened by experience. Conscience-bound by puritanism, instinctively a creature of the flesh, and self-reproachful on both accounts, he begins his solitary walk of "the present" and experiences, typically, an urge to move off the well trodden path. Interior monologue tells us that he is afraid to do so, because he might get lost and there would be nobody to help. There, at once, is the gist of the film: precisely the same challenge that was taken up by the women in Malle's *Les Amants* and the Resnais masterpiece *L'Année dernière à Marienbad*, when those two films ended with the abandonment of security for the possible but doubtful fulfilment of desire. In this sense, and with the interesting difference that the key figure is a man, *Kungsleden* begins where Malle and Resnais stopped. Du, on his wishful and reproachful journey, will take no photographs to show his wife and children when he goes home again: as he explains to a German tourist he meets in passing, "This time, I am walking for myself."

It is a walk he owes himself: a suspenseful elegy: the puritan's lament for the primitive, the romantic's ineradicable urge to clutch at the unattainable.

7. Among Thieves

A CERTAIN affection for thieves is taken for granted. Even when they kill, if interrupted perchance in the course of a robbery, their "reason" for killing is self-evident at once: their psychological demands upon the spectator are less arduous than those of the insane killers for whom compassion must be cultivated rather delicately. Thieves are manifestly courageous, and their nerves of steel are not necessarily allied to heads of bone, because robbery calls for a spot of ingenuity. In the generalised terms of the cinema norm, thieves are romantic. To the spectator who does a routine job to earn his living, their brave bids for rich gain are enviable. Perhaps a latent anarchy is indulged vicariously. The spectator, bound by society's rules, is permitted the luxury of identifying for a time with those who break the bonds. The fact that they rarely get away with the spoils, and that retribution is virtually inevitable in the cinema, enables the wishful dreamer to adjust at the fade-out, with any luck. Reconciled to his humble lot, he sees the disadvantage of emulation. Without the necessary luck, things might be otherwise in individual cases. Therefore it becomes obligatory for the film-maker to emphasise the retribution as clearly as he has conveyed the dangerous zest of the robbery.

The loner among thieves of the cinema will provoke sympathetic suspense. Safe-cracking *Raffles* has been romantically incarnated by John Barrymore (1917), House Peters (1925), Ronald Colman (1930), and David Niven (1939). The more memorable film robberies, however, are perpetrated by groups of men. Operations are planned with military precision. There is a bitter parallel with the teamwork of war.

A disadvantage of the group robbery is the instructional period, redolent of the classroom, anti-cinematic, and sometimes even involving maps or diagrams. Members of the group are briefed, and so, simultaneously, is the spectator. The more complex the plan, the more long-winded the preparatory gen. The counter-measure to this impediment is lively dialogue for sharply defined characters within the group, as in Basil Dearden's *The League of Gentlemen* (1959; screenplay by Bryan Forbes, from a novel by John Boland). This is, of course, a comedy: the more notable because good comedy dialogue is pretty rare, and the feat of combining it with detailed information is even rarer. More effective still, if easier, is the broader eccentricity of the instructional sequence in Alexander Mackendrick's *The Ladykillers* (1955),

"Conveniently deep
shadow"—THE BEAST
WITH FIVE FINGERS.

where the robbery plan is less complicated and can be com-
bined with some comic darting about: the robbers, equipped
with musical instruments, are pretending to be members of a
string quartet, and play a gramophone record to delude the
landlady but are flummoxed when she comes up to the room
to offer them tea. In serious films about group robbery, however, the planning sequences are boring but necessary evils to
be dealt with as quickly as possible.

A worse impediment, as far as suspense is concerned, is
the cosiness of group activity. The loner's evocation of tension is dissipated by weight of numbers. At the scene of the
robbery itself, we are not concentrating upon one isolated
and vulnerable individual but upon the teamwork of a unified
little band. However much at loggerheads the individual
members of the group might be, their joint interest will unite
them while the job is being done; so, in the robbery scene,
suspense must arise from situation entirely, without the
added suspense factor of "identification" with one specific
character. The robbery in The League of Gentlemen, a
sprightly business, is carried out under a smokescreen with
the participants wearing gas masks. The situation itself is very
holding and very cinematic, but the spectator can barely tell
which thief is which.

Looked upon with objectivity, as filmic patterns of movement, group robberies can be notable set pieces. One such is
the factory payroll robbery in Robert Siodmak's The Killers
(1946), with its smooth and flowing crane shot as the group
moves across the factory yard and converges upon the build-

ing, mounting an iron staircase, and then walking quickly along a landing: the effect is virtually choreographic, the movement followed at a cool remove by a camera which imparts to the spectator a sense of levitation.

In Jean-Pierre Melville's *Le deuxième souffle* (1966) a van is waylaid and relieved of its cargo of platinum on a twisting mountain road in the vicinity of Toulon. The operation is carried out by four gangsters. The technique is exceptional in its swift-changing compositions, its neat incorporation of zoom shots, and its keenly-timed cutting. Suspense builds steadily during the period of waiting for the van and its police escort to come into sight. From a position on a rocky hill overlooking the hairpin bend where the van is to be held up, one of the four men fixes the vital area in his gunsights. The others just wait. Percussion on the soundtrack, having contributed its quota to the tension, stops abruptly. Now we can hear the drone of the mistral. Through a small triangular gap in the rocks, a forward zoom gives us our first sight of the approaching van: a helmeted policeman rides in front of it on a motorcycle, and another follows behind the van. From the elevated view through the gap, Melville cuts to a moderately close shot of the first policeman, and then a backward zoom includes the van in the frame as well. Next, a cut to the interior of the van, its comparative darkness making an immediate contrast to the sunlit exteriors: a panning shot takes in the platinum and the man who guards it. In the next exterior, the camera travels backwards before the advancing van and escort, giving place shortly to another view from the gunsights above. Momentarily, as a bullet hits the policeman who rides in front, the screen is flooded with whiteness. The policeman on his motorcycle veers off the road and hurtles downhill. The killings are over quickly. The boxes of platinum are unloaded by the gangsters, whose faces are covered now by white masks. The van is pushed over a cliff: a slow downward pan as it crumbles and disintegrates carries a hint of inevitability. The four gangsters look down from the edge of the cliff: they stand, backs to camera, in an orderly line to the left of the frame, wearing formal black overcoats, a firmly defined group against the prevailing white in the composition. Presently the group is broken up as the men move away from the cliff-top toward waiting cars. They walk with the determined precision of purposeful dogs.

Suspense has been derived entirely from incident, despite the fact that each of the four gangsters has been established already as an individual character. We know nothing of the victims, although we learn afterwards that the two motorcycle policemen had wives and children. It is therefore impersonal suspense. Palpably keener, however, is the suspense when the central character, the gangster Gus (Lino Ventura), is alone again. He walks along a tree-lined street in Marseilles, the camera travelling a little ahead of him. The only other people in our field of vision are two lovers under a tree. We see no more than Gus himself is aware of, yet we scent a certain menace, implicit in the isolation of Gus. As he advances, the camera moves obliquely toward him until his profile is in close-up. At this moment, abruptly, a hand enters the frame from the right and presses a revolver to the back of his neck.

Later in the film, this position is stylishly reversed when Gus is able to gain the upper hand. The camera holds the profile of a police inspector in close-up as he drives his car along a deserted road. A hand enters the frame, this time from the left, applying the revolver-to-neck shock. The revolver is held by Gus, who has been concealed in the back of the inspector's car.

The criminal *milieu* of *Le deuxième souffle*, and of several other Melville films, is imbued with romantic ivory-tower ethics. The anarchistic characters observe their own code of honour in a half-world between dignity and sentimentality. The same is true of the criminals in Jules Dassin's *Du rififi chez les hommes* (1954). Here too is a remarkable group robbery sequence, enacted without dialogue and with only minimal use of incidental sounds, and lasting for about half an hour. Its impact is due in no small measure to the unusually long absence of speech. Four men rob a jewellery shop in Paris. Their plan, highly detailed, begins with the drilling of a hole in the floor of the room above the one they need to enter. When a small hole has been made, an umbrella is inserted through it. With the handle secure in the upper room, the umbrella is opened beneath the ceiling of the lower room in order to catch falling plaster as the hole is enlarged sufficiently to let a man descend. So it goes on, in acute tension. Yet, good as this is, the climax of the entire film is able to exceed it in suspense by focusing attention upon a single individual in a desperate situation. He is the leader of the group, Tony le Stéphanois (Jean Servais), whose tubercular condition, the result of five years in prison, is an incidental bid for the spectator's sympathy. One of his men has been killed by a rival gang, and the young son of this man is being held for ransom, to be exchanged for the loot from the robbery. After much gunfire in the tradition of gangster movies, which never attain the *brio* of equivalent occasions in westerns, Tony retrieves the child but is so badly wounded himself that his fast drive through Paris to possible safety is charged with suspense. The child in the car is unaware of the danger as Tony strives to retain consciousness at the wheel. In a style judiciously pitched between routine realism and melodrama, the ride of Tony le Stéphanois is a memorable accomplishment.

Of course, given only two crooks, as for example in Henri

Verneuil's *Mélodie en sous-sol* (1962; re-titled *The Big Snatch* in the U.K. and *Any Number Can Win* in the U.S.), it is possible to combine a suspense arising from the characters with the tension of situation as the deed is done. The mastermind of this robbery is Charles (Jean Gabin), an old hand who is feeling the weight of his years and is anxious to make one big *coup* before retiring. He requires a partner younger than himself, because physical agility is involved, so he chooses a smooth blade by the name of Francis (Alain Delon) whose acquaintance he has made during a spell in prison. It proves to be an uneasy combination. Charles, forever calm but nevertheless wary, is inclined to think as time goes on that the flippant and self-indulgent ways of Francis might jeopardise the scheme. For practical reasons, conflict between the two is held at bay, generating its suspense the while; and the continuing uncertainty of Charles is carried over into the robbery sequence, when Francis for his part is an isolated adventurer who must squirm through air-conditioning ducts and lower himself down a lift well.

The sweaty doings are successful, but retribution ensues at dawn. Since the police are converging, Francis has deposited two suitcases full of stolen banknotes in a swimming pool. The partners sit on opposite sides of the pool, pretending not to know one another. The early sun offers Charles an excuse to wear dark glasses. His face is a study in the concealment of frustration as the police approach and simultaneously the water erodes the suitcases and the banknotes float upward until the entire surface of the pool is carpeted dankly with evidence of the crime.

8. By Accident

THE unpredictable element, so prevalent in life, can be manipulated cunningly in films, to tighten the screw of suspense.

An early John Sturges film, *Jeopardy* (1952), scripted by Mel Dinelli from a story by Maurice Zimm, is a masterly little essay in suspense built upon accident: the misfortunes arise because the two leading characters, one after the other, find themselves in the wrong place at the wrong time. Helen (Barbara Stanwyck) and her husband Doug (Barry Sullivan) are on holiday in Mexico with their young son, Bobby (Lee Aaker). On a remote beach, which they have to themselves, the child prowls about under a decrepit jetty at low tide, and jams his foot between a couple of planks. Doug manages to get him loose, but in the process he brings down part of the jetty and is trapped beneath heavy timber. Helen cannot move it. In four hours the tide will be high. Already a wave is lapping at Doug's feet. Leaving Bobby with Doug, Helen takes the car and goes heading into the second accidental circumstance. At a deserted petrol station, she looks for a rope to tie to the timbers, but she is set upon suddenly by an escaped convict, Lawson (Ralph Meeker), who makes her drive him away from the Mexican police who are chasing him. She tries to brake the car at a road block, but Lawson compels her to drive right through it. Presently a tyre gives out.

89

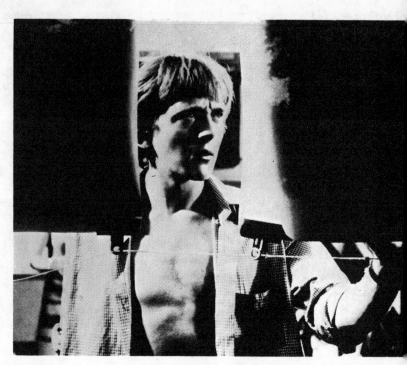

"Mystery without solution"—David Hemmings in BLOW-UP.

Lawson puts on the spare, and Helen tries to knock him out with a wrench, unsuccessfully. Failing that, she makes him a proposition: if he will rescue Doug, he can take Doug's clothes and identity papers, and, moreover, Helen herself will gratify him sexually, even to the extent of going off with him and abandoning her husband. Lawson accepts this generous offer.

Thus far the events might well seem a bit "far-fetched", though never less than plausible. Vital to their holding power, never giving the spectator time to quibble, is the pace: the duration of the entire film is sixty-nine minutes. Also it was already apparent then that John Sturges is a director with a very keen flair for composition, imparting drama through the visual impact: a talent that was to be affirmed subsequently in *Bad Day at Black Rock*, *Gunfight at the OK Corral* and *Last Train from Gun Hill* with their memorable patterns of figures in arid landscapes and their tough-balletic sense of movement. Given the swift incidents of Helen's accidental encounter with Lawson, the slow agony of Doug carries its simultaneous tension, which could be expressed quite succinctly in visual terms. A lobster boat is sighted from the beach. Bobby cries out to it, but is not heard. The tide rises relentlessly until only Doug's head is clear of the water.

When Helen and Lawson get there, a powerful attempt on Lawson's part to move the timber from Doug is unsuccessful, so he takes Doug's identity papers out of his pocket and makes off. But Helen attacks him fist and claw, until he tries again. This time Doug is set free. The end is nimble: Lawson is so lost in admiration of Helen's pluck that he does not hold her to the bargain.

There is double-accident value, too, in Louis Malle's *Ascenseur pour l'échafaud* (1957), from a novel by Noël Calef. In an office building in Paris, the electricity is shut off for the night, causing a lift to stop between floors. The lift happens to be occupied by a man who has just murdered his employer in the same building. Again, the trapped man (Maurice Ronet) can be shown in occasional telling visuals, suggesting the dangerous passing of quite a long period of time while, in fact, occupying very little actual screen time. Against his claustrophobic predicament is set the agoraphobic quest of the woman who is expecting him to meet her (Jeanne Moreau). She is the widow of the murdered man. Her wanderings through the ironic-poetic Paris night are cross-cut with the lover's debilitating condition in the lift and his eventual discovery that he can take up part of the floor and lower himself down the well of the lift on a cable. In the middle of this nervy feat, a nightwatchman in the lobby below drops his keys and switches on the electricity in order to find them. The lift begins to move downwards, carrying the man on the cable toward a disaster that is averted at the traditional last moment when the nightwatchman finds his keys and switches the current off.

The second accidental circumstance, to which the film is building simultaneously in another cross-cut phase of the story, occurs when a rebellious and edgy young boy shoots a German tourist at a motel. This boy has stolen the parked car of the man in the lift, and, as a consequence, the light of dawn sees the man accused of murder: not the murder he has committed, but the murder of the German. The richness of this irony through accidental events is only slightly diminished by an implausible ending in which the truth of the matter is unearthed by the police.

Deeper strains are evident. The initial murderer is an ex-paratrooper, employing his acquired skill to a personal rather than patriotic end. The young boy is an impulse killer, anti-social on account of his inability to adjust to a life that seems persistently to thwart him. The subtle night-poetry prefigures variations on this visual and psychological theme in subsequent Malle films, and notably in his master-piece *Le feu follet* (1963). At the time when *Ascenseur pour l'échafaud* had established him as a young director of great promise, Malle declared, "I will not make another 'thriller' for a long time, but I hope to come back to, and develop, certain ideas outlined in this first film: a certain indifference to killing and to letting oneself kill; the hard and inhuman aspect of the modern world; solitude, separation, searching . . . and the night." *

It is often the case, as in both *Jeopardy* and *Ascenseur pour l'échafaud*, that the element of chance can provide suspense without the more common ingredient of mystery. As Hitch-cock has said, "Sometimes the audience will sweat more if there is no mystery." * In this context, Anatole Litvak's *The Night of the Generals* (1966) is interesting to contemplate. Once into its stride, it had no mystery, although it rather pretended that it did. Its vital "accidental" climax, when Grau (Omar Sharif) is killed by Tanz (Peter O'Toole), is reached by the eventual overlapping of two threads of plot which for quite a long time seem almost unrelated to one another. The waywardness of real life, contained within a professionally-knit plot structure, impinges most persuasively and dramatically after a build-up that seems constantly in danger of losing its suspense but never quite does.

General Tanz is a psychopathic Nazi who relishes the duty-killing of wartime, and also indulges privately, at well-spaced intervals, in the brutal killing of prostitutes. At the climax in question, he is on the point of being arrested for his private murders by the intelligence officer Grau. The moment is so arranged that Tanz is able to shoot Grau in the name of duty, on the pretext that Grau has been involved in the abortive conspiracy of certain German officers to assassinate Hitler in July of 1944.

The screenplay, from the novel by Hans Hellmut Kirst, gravitates toward this climax by shifting attention, quite arbitrarily, back and forth between the central core of the drama, the murders committed privately by Tanz, and the seemingly irrelevant development of the scheme to kill Hitler. Two suspenseful situations are in hand, cross-cut, but hardly making a clear-cut progression in the orthodox thriller manner; and it is in this very divergence from a norm we are conditioned to expect in thrillers that the strange, if somewhat awkward, power of the film resides.

The main thread, the tracking down of a murderer, has plenty of nuance, especially in respect of the investigator Grau: a rum little number, he. As to Tanz, emphatically insane, there are but muted hints of the motivation specified in the novel: spite engendered by homosexual frustration. Clearer is the echo of Kirst's denigration of war-training as a breeding ground for the killer instinct. A deposition in the novel states the point: "War is to crime what the coming of spring is to a garden." The novel also presents Tanz as "the personification of war—of a war which was nothing more nor less than a cruel, pointless, uncontrolled blood-bath"; the killer-general's face is "merely the mask of war, an iron mask concealing blood-lust, destruction—perhaps even, Hell itself." The film conveys all this, not least through the acting of O'Toole, judging the hazards of big-screen close-ups to a nicety and overstating only to the degree consistent with the mental and emotional condition of Tanz.

Our understanding toward Tanz, as distinct from sympathy for him, is elicited in two passages that have been admirably translated from novel to film, where he visits a collection of paintings in Paris and stands transfixed before a self-portrait of the insane Van Gogh. On both occasions, the first shock bringing on a near-faint and the second compulsive view having the same effect but this time with the added element of instinctive self-torture, we are informed discomfortingly of Tanz's dreadful awareness of his own malaise. He contrives to endure his madness by consuming large quantities of cognac, which he holds well; and also by regimenting his life to a fanatical degree, which is not so fanatical as to be unidentifiable with that common desire for orderly routines, tidy filing systems, neat desktops, and the other varied disciplines that are not merely practical but superficially consoling, implying as they do that we have our affairs under control. Tanz is so well organised that he can regulate his outlets, and bottle up his lust until the rare and fairly safe occasions when it can be indulged. Even then he is disciplined enough to balk at the prospect of a day or two off duty, knowing what the inevitable result will be: one more private murder.

Opposed to him, Grau is on the face of it a crusading avenger. Yet, in both novel and film, he is an ambiguous character, outwardly cool, inwardly savouring the lust of the chase. A French police inspector, with whom he consults and bargains suavely, informs him of the plot to kill Hitler. Grau's indifferent response surprises the Frenchman: "I tell you about a plot, and you show no interest, but if I can help you to solve the murder of a whore you are delighted." To which Grau replies: "I've no sense of proportion; it's been pointed out to me before." And later in the same conversation he says, "I'm interested in just one general who killed a girl and thought, because he was a general, he could play God in bed as well as in battle. Well, I'm going to demonstrate to him that he is not God." "And that you *are*?" "My madness is on a smaller, more secular scale. I simply want to see justice done." The expression of this sentiment is pat, even pi. The point about the individual life mattering, at a time when killing on a massive scale is prevalent, is one of the film's major affirmations. But the work as a whole is more complex. Grau, beneath his diplomatic charm, is driven by a vengeance-compulsion as persistent as the urge that forces Tanz to murder.

The shape of the plot, and the Hitler cross-plot, is unorthodox and quite absorbing. At the beginning of the film there is mystery. We gather that the murderer is one of three generals. But before very long the film is concentrating so emphatically upon the character of Tanz that there is very little room in our minds for doubt. Once he has made his

94

first reaction to the Van Gogh, the genre has changed from whodunnit to case history. Then the Hitler cross-plot is introduced, quietly and dramatically, during a stroll in a garden at the Paris residence of General von Stulpnagel. It is our first intimation that this slice of fact is to be interwoven with the fiction. The weaving is not of the smoothest, perhaps; and in this matter one notes the distinction between novel and film. Kirst's compelling book, leading us back and forth from Tanz plot to Hitler plot, is something for the contemplative mood. Like all books, it is unlikely to be read from cover to cover without interruption. A film is viewed all the way through at a sitting. This gives it the advantage of concentrated attention from the spectator, but also an obligation to hold that attention. Lunging on, as it were, and unable to turn back a reel as one turns back a page, the spectator can easily loose the thread, or find himself perplexed at the sudden appearance of such a divergent thread as this one of the Hitler plot. The novel, save for its interpolated depositions supposedly given at a later period in time by people who could throw light on the events, is orientated in Paris, with the main Tanz plot, at the time when the Hitler cross-plot begins. The progress of the attempted assassination of Hitler is disclosed by indirect report. Not so in the film, which takes full advantage of its ability to "show", and dramatises visually the bomb incident at Hitler's hut in Rastenburg.

There is some to and fro-ing between plot and cross-plot, to be sure, but I should have preferred it faster. After that initial information in the Paris garden, we are transported to the western front, where Rommel is virtually dragged into the film. The transition is smooth, on account of a carry-over narration. This is a direct cut, with no time lapse, from the garden to Rommel's tent, which we can see already while Stulpnagel's voice (carried over from the garden scene) is saying "When we need him he will join us here." The plan of the conspiring officers to make Rommel president of the German republic that would replace Hitler is of minimal importance in the context of the film, yet we stay with Rommel through an episode in which planes attack his car and he is wounded. All of this carries us wildly away from the main plot, but we return to it eventually with a good scene, expanding dramatically and visually from the novel, in which Tanz goes to a nightclub and is encountered by a blonde, whom he disdains pointedly, but whom he will pick up and murder the following evening. We stay with Tanz until he makes his second visit to the Van Gogh, and then the film remains orientated in Paris, with second-hand news of the Hitler doings, which seems more apt, and the main plot continues to the point where the blonde is murdered. After this comes the enactment, which is very holding, of the Stauffenberg venture with the bomb in the Rastenburg hut. The cross-cutting now is cautious, but it draws its comparison between one kind of killing and another. As Stauffenberg approaches the hut where Hitler is in conference, there is a cut to the apartment of the murdered girl in Paris. Grau and the French police inspector are looking at the body. Grau says that he is determined to arrest whichever general is responsible, and the Frenchman expresses the view that this would be ill-timed, because, as they both know, that day is "Doomsday". The word is the cue for a cut to the conference at Rastenburg. Stauffenberg puts his briefcase, with the bomb in it, under the table and makes an excuse to leave the room. Another cut back to Paris: Grau is trying to talk to one of the other generals he suspects of the murder, but this man is up to his neck in the conspiracy against Hitler, and his pre-occupation with that transfers us to Rastenburg again. Stauffenberg is well away from the hut when it blows up, and is confident that Hitler must be dead. So we return to Paris, and stay there while rumblings of the cross-plot continue very dramatically as Grau becomes firmly convinced that, of the three generals he suspects, Tanz is the murderer.

It is here that the two threads meet, in a fine flourish of melodrama, and excellent melodrama at that. Grau accuses Tanz, when they are alone, of murdering two prostitutes: the first, two years before in Warsaw, and the second just the previous evening in Paris. A radio is heard, reporting that the attempt on Hitler's life has failed. Tanz shoots Grau; and when an officer comes running at the sound of the shot, Tanz tells him that Grau was in league with the conspirators.

(From this climax, the film nimbly leaps twenty years to a third prostitute murder in Hamburg and the delayed retribution: the French police inspector completes Grau's unfinished task, but, humanely, permits Tanz to commit suicide.)

The Night of the Generals is a handsome looking film, of rather conventional technique. In terms of plot construction, it is unorthodox. Setting aside the profusion of other characters, each with a specific individual purpose in the complicated story, it can be seen broadly as a four-part construction. Part one is murder mystery, backgrounded by a certain amount of wartime detail. Parts two and three, overlapping, give us the Tanz case-history and the Hitler cross-plot. Part four, relatively short, is an epilogue which unifies the whole thing by having Grau's obsessive quest (the sustained factor throughout every part of the film except the Hitler cross-plot) completed after his death. It does not seem this neat on an initial viewing, nor should it, because the Hitler cross-plot really needs to be as apart from the central core as possible, not only to gain the maximum surprise impact from the killing of Grau (with its convincingly accidental note of the radio announcement being heard at just that moment), but also to indicate that in life one neat train of events is apt at any moment to be influenced by quite another set of circumstances.

A criticism levelled at the film was that the identity of the murderer could be guessed quite early in the piece. It would have been better, I think, to have made no bones about this: as it stands, when the spectator is firmly convinced that Tanz is the man, Grau is given a line to the effect that perhaps this solution to the mystery would be too obvious, thereby casting doubt again for a time, but to no good purpose. Indeed, the spectator conditioned to murder mysteries could well be irritated to realise that his first thought had been right, after that line of Grau's had prepared him for a more customary revelation of a villain unsuspected.

All the same, it is salutary from time to time to disconcert the conditioned spectator. A film that solves its mystery unexpectedly soon is to that extent daring, while one that presents a mystery and never solves it is apt to upset many people in a way that can do them good. Again it is a case of recognising that life does not have the neatness of a machine-tooled plot. Some answers are never known. On occasion, the unsolved mystery can bring about other conditions that become the main theme of a film. In Mervyn Le Roy's *They Won't Forget* (1937), a young girl (Lana Turner) is murdered in one of the southern states of the U.S.A. This happens early in the film and is foreshadowed by a memorably nervy sequence where the girl walks through an empty street while the festive sounds of a parade are heard in the distance. Obviously the whole town is there, and nobody is here in the street except the girl. Her isolation and vulnerability are unsettling. The impression is that of a thriller, and, as investigations ensue, the conditioned spectator might expect that eventually the murderer will be revealed. This never happens. A northerner in town, the girl's schoolteacher (Edward Norris), is the favourite suspect because prejudice against northerners runs high. A shrewd and ruthless district attorney (Claude Rains) makes out a strong case against the northerner and upholds it with histrionic fervour in court. Afterwards, the northerner is lynched, and in the final scene the district attorney admits privately that he does not know whether the man was guilty or not. The indictment of prejudice has outweighed the mystery element, although, for the benefit of those who like to do their own detecting, Le Roy included a close shot, at the time of the girl's solitary walk, of an elderly party who ogled her in such a way as to afford a possible "solution".

A mystery without solution is instrumental to the theme of disorientation in Antonioni's *Blow-up* (1966). Thomas, a young professional photographer (David Hemmings), wants to take a quiet idyllic picture that will offset the harshness of the reality depicted in a book of photographs he is about to have published. He goes into a park. Our first sight of this park is restricted: trees near the entrance, in a quiet backwater of London: trees disturbed by the wind, a distinct threat in the sound, suggesting that things might not be as idyllic as he hopes. In the park he takes numerous photographs of a girl and an older man, possibly lovers. The girl (Vanessa Redgrave) sees Thomas and runs across to him to demand the negatives. He refuses, and continues to photo-

98

graph her as she runs away. Apparently the man she was with has gone already. Later, after developing the photographs, Thomas gazes curiously at one of them, and then makes a blow-up of a segment of it, and studies a shape in the bushes some little distance away from the couple. This shape looks like a gun, pointing toward the pair. A blow-up of another segment, from one of the photographs taken as the girl was running away, discloses what might be a body at the foot of a tree. Later still, when night has fallen, Thomas goes back to that place in the park, and beneath the tree he sees (or appears to see) the dead body of the man the girl had been talking to when he took the photographs. He returns home to find that the blow-ups have been stolen. After a night of indecision, during which he indulges in drugs, he returns to the park at dawn. There is no body at the foot of the tree. Perhaps there never was.

A previous Antonioni mystery without solution is to be found in *L'Avventura* (1960). As in the case of *Blow-up*, this mystery is relevant to the film, but the solution of it is not. Indeed, the absence of a solution is part of the point: life's uncertainty. The girl (Lea Massari) who disappears mysteriously from an island in *L'Avventura* is sought in vain, if with diminishing zeal, throughout the greater part of the film.

Perhaps she has committed suicide, perhaps not. The purpose of her disappearance, as I construe it, is to serve as an irritant to the consciences of the two lovers (Monica Vitti and Gabriele Ferzetti) whose difficult liaison is the principal subject of the work. The conscience of Thomas in *Blow-up* is not troubled by any sense of obligation or responsibility to the girl he has photographed in the park. Human relationships do not go very deep with Thomas. Selfish and self-tormented, he draws what confidence he can from the mastery he has over his camera. Yet his blow-ups of the pictures from the park disclose that the camera has possibly functioned independently, in the sense that there is more in the photographs than Thomas realised when he took them. Thus his mastery is called into question.

At first he is intrigued, curous; something of the amateur detective. He wants to discover the hidden truth in a situation that had seemed to him both commonplace and pleasant, and was photographed as such. His curiosity is a kind of awakening, a tentative step toward involvement with the world that exists outside himself. He is quite young, and he lives in a period (the 1960s) when many of his contemporaries have gravitated from protest into apathy. He is not quite of their number. Apathy is held at bay by a nagging discontent, with himself, with his life. He has a deal in common with other male characters in the films of Antonioni, the important difference being that he is younger. Well-heeled, discontented, realising that material advantages have been gained at the expense of ideals, he is young enough to feel that there is still time to do something to redress the balance. On the material plane he works hard, earning big money from fashion photography, acquiring property, using his talent and his wits, ruthlessly, even desperately, while at the same time reaching out rather blindly toward spiritual fulfilment. This eludes him, partly, on account of the deliberate barrier he has set up between himself and other people, dehumanising himself in order to get on as quickly and profitably as possible with his working life. Thus sex, always a prime factor in Antonioni films, is for Thomas a strictly physical incidental in the process of living: it is always around for the choosing, and his choice is made as casually and quickly as his selection of food

"Forbidding territory"—ROBINSON CRUSOE ON MARS.

in a tolerable restaurant. The new element of his amateur detective work, then, is a kind of turning-point. The true suspense resides not in the mystery of the blow-ups but in the instability of Thomas himself.

As Thomas pins up his enlarged segments of the photographs that were taken in the park, and the camera roves across them, a miniature drama emerges from concealment. Back and forth the camera moves, from the image of what might be a gun in the bushes to the smudge that might be a body by the tree. The reliability of these images is in doubt. The bigger the blow-up, the less distinct the outlines. A painter has remarked to Thomas that long after he has completed an abstract canvas he will gaze at it and suddenly a pattern will emerge. The significance or "meaning" of the pattern is a matter for individual conjecture. One cannot say for sure just what it means or even what it is; and in a world that hankers after the certainty of facts, this inability to be sure is difficult for many to accept. We don't know, therefore we fear.

The thriller-suspense of discovery, or imagined discovery,

101

in the blow-up sequence, sparking a reaction to supposed reality in Thomas, is followed up by his supposed verification when he sees the body that night beneath the tree in the park. He is convinced that he has seen it. Our view of it is subjective: we see what he sees. But we must remember that he is emotionally and mentally insecure, and capable of willing himself to see in his mind's eye a "fact" of which he has convinced himself before he goes back to the park. Doubt ensues for Thomas: with the disappearances of the blow-ups from his studio and the body from the park.

Of course, for comfort, we can make up explanations. The girl's determination to obtain the negatives, and the theft of the blow-ups, could imply an embarrassing liaison between her and the man she was with in the park. If he is not dead, but merely ran away in panic, then perhaps the girl herself, or a friend, or even the man himself, could have broken in and taken the blow-ups because they made that liaison all too plain. Perhaps the man was married, perhaps the girl was married; perhaps her lover or husband was in the bushes with the gun, and, if so, perhaps this murderer returned in the small hours to get rid of the corpse. We don't know. And the reason we don't know is that Thomas doesn't know. Our lack of certainty about "facts" enables us to understand his frustration. He has reached beyond his material world with confidence in the camera he thinks he masters. He would probably not be so foolish as to think that his camera never lies; but he does think that he controls it, and, while sometimes he might require it to lie, in this case he intended it to picture the truth. The initial curiosity, the amateur-detecting, suggested progress, a move toward involvement and adjustment as distinct from the hyper-cool detachment he has cultivated as a means of what Thurber called "getting through the day". Now, trying to appease the artist in him, as the fruits of his materialism have enabled him to do, he has taken time off from the remunerative artificiality of fashion photography, sought out "truth" and arrived at uncertainty.

The real suspense, maintained until the final scene, is his interior battle to adjust and survive, to live with the knowledge that sometimes, and perhaps quite often, there are no explanations. If the gun and the body in the blow-ups are

102

. . . to murder and be done with it"— Edward G. Robinson with (above) Dame May (?)y and (below) Aubrey Smith FLESH AND FANTASY.

facts, they are very indistinct; if the corpse under the tree is a real corpse, the light of dawn makes one doubt. For a time, the saving grace of curiosity has sustained Thomas. It is his native, human reaction against the unknown. But subsequently truth is too elusive, and the unknown is unbearable. The easy way now, the consoling way, is to assume that he has imagined everything. Mercifully for him, yet sadly too, it is made easy by example: fantasy is to hand, represented by a group of revellers. This same group appeared at the very beginning of the film, riding in a jeep, garishly attired, their faces painted white in the fashion of mimes. Their first appearance, conflicting with the impersonal modernity of city buildings, was by way of prelude. Young, like Thomas, they have opted out of the real world, perhaps for a short therapeutic period or perhaps for ever. Returning to the film, as it closes, they disport themselves, harmlessly and happily, on a vacant tennis court. They pretend a game, going through the motions without ball or rackets. Thomas watches, in a kind of envy. One mime-player hits the non-existent ball over the fence, and Thomas is asked to pick it up and throw it back. He does this, and continues to watch. We see only Thomas now, his eyes following the ball back and forth. For him, the ball is real. Just as we saw the corpse beneath the tree when Thomas saw it, we hear now the sound of racket hitting ball. Like a boon, or a blight, fantasy has gained control. Thomas disappears. His image dissolves, until only the grass he was standing on fills the screen. His retreat from reality is complete. As a creature of the factual world, he exists no longer.

However the moral is meant by Antonioni himself, interpretation rests with the spectator, as is the case in many films of depth, not least those of Hitchcock. The suspense of Thomas might have been resolved happily, with a determination to maintain equilibrium somewhere between the creative world of the imagination and the ulcerated area of materialism and fact. Since it is not resolved happily, but rather in a total surrender to fantasy and consequently to oblivion, we can take it either as an exhortation to come to terms with reality, or as a cautionary tale in which the pursuit of material gain is a threat to humanity.

The "detective" phase, in its familiar place in thriller cinema, might still have a significance greater than the manner of a fairly routine film would suggest. Herbert Mason's *A Window in London* (1940), for example: Peter (Michael Redgrave), on his way to work by train, can see from the train window a man stabbing a girl at the window of a house the train is passing; he tells the police, investigations are made, and it turns out that the pair are music-hall artists rehearsing their act. By the end of the film, however, events have come to such a pass that the murder imagined by Peter really takes place. Ironically he smiles as his train passes the same house again, little knowing that beyond the window the girl lies dead.

Such an ending can be accepted as wry, or pondered in relationship to the elusive nature of truth: a matter richly explored in Akira Kurosawa's *Rashomon* (1950), with its four separate and contradictory accounts of the same murder, any or none of which might be true. Each account is coloured by the self-interest and pride of the person who relates it. Certain facts are clear: a woman has been raped, a man is dead. But the real truth of the matter is clouded (perhaps unintentionally), because people have a way of interpreting things so as to represent their own personalities to the best advantage. The feat of Kurosawa's film (maintained in Martin Ritt's 1965 version, *The Outrage*, which transposed the setting from old Japan to the American west of the 1880s) is to keep the spectator expectant throughout four flashbacks that show the same situation with subtle variations. There is double suspense: that of wondering how things will vary each time, and that of trying to determine which version is the true one. The fact that the spectator never finds out is a pertinent fact. It makes the film's point: one man's truth is different from another's.

We arrive therefore at what might be termed an accident of nature: concepts of reality will vary according to individual dispositions. The spectator watching Clouzot's *Le salaire de la peur* (1953) for the first time will in all probability accept it as realism unadulterated, whereas in retrospect it strains credulity beyond the limits. It is, of course, a masterpiece of suspense, affirming Clouzot's stature and command, and above all his impeccable sense of timing which is the open secret of its power to persuade.

Somewhere in central America an oil well is on fire, and an explosion of nitro-glycerine is needed to put out the monstrous blaze. Representatives of the American oil company recruit four men from a seedy and impoverished little community to transport the stuff in two trucks for several hundred miles over rough country. The chances of accident are high, but the monetary rewards are great and especially tempting to the destitute men who undertake the task.

(Negotiations are conducted in such a manner as to suggest that American capitalism is heartless, a peripheral and somewhat laboured aspect which stirred up a flurry of political controversy when the film was projected at the Cannes festival: one of a number of things that are wrong with film festivals is that politics will tend to intrude drearily upon the more important terrain of art.)

A small explosion is heard as a tiny drop of the nitroglycerine is spilled. The way ahead of the drivers is full of ruts and treacherous roads around mountains: much of the filming was done on location to the north of Nimes. Accidents loom, and each one of them is overcome by one of the trucks, although the other meets its doom en route and the occasion is marked by a masterstroke on Clouzot's part when the distant blast sets up a wind that reaches far enough to blow the tobacco from a cigarette being rolled by one of the men in the other truck. This other truck is the centre of our attention (and let it be said that Yves Montand and Charles Vanel play its frightened drivers superbly). Considered singly, each dilemma faced is plausible enough. Coming in quantity, they make one doubt that any driver could have survived so much. The doubt comes afterwards, not while the film is going on. The style is classic, even austere in respect of camerawork. Clouzot followed the time-honoured principle of placing the shocks between relatively quiet passages ("*les pointes extrêmes du drame étant séparées par des zones neutres*"). It is a dubious principle, because in run-of-the-mill stories the "*zones neutres*" are just plain dull and the "*pointes extrêmes*" stick out like sensationally sore thumbs. The holding power of the circumstances in *Le salaire de la peur* obviated the first of these problems: knowing that something accidental could threaten the men at any moment, the spectator never lapsed into a "*zone neutre*" of his own. Of course, the "*pointes extrêmes*" were highly sensational, but here the timing of Clouzot came into its own. Take just one incident, when the truck has to be turned around on a fragile wooden platform that extends from the edge of a steep mountain. As the truck is manœuvred, the structure begins to give way. The cutting is classic, bringing in details of the weakening supports of the platform, which

106

"The reborn"—
Rock Hudson in
SECONDS.

collapses and falls in a shambles down the mountainside at the precise moment when the truck is safely back on the road. The thing is absurd in terms of realism. It is the accentuated fear of the silent clowns. Harry Langdon, in *Tramp, Tramp, Tramp* (1926, directed by Harry Edwards) clings to a fence that is collapsing on the edge of a precipice, and nails his sweater to the fence for extra support, all the time pulling nails out of the posts that hold the fence in place: the close detailed shots of nails being removed are a direct and classic parallel to Clouzot's cutting in the mountainside sequence.

Yet one laughs at Langdon's plight, but not at the predicament of Montand and Vanel. The reason is hardly to be found in the story, for all its inherent seriousness. At the *"pointe extrême"* a reaction laugh would be likely, were it not for the uncanny timing, the instinctive knowledge of just how long to hold each single shot before replacing it with the next, and how to build this montage of images with a precision that virtually brain-washes the spectator into the belief that this impossible "event" is not a cinematic contrivance but something that is actually happening as he watches it. The technique is old and often used. Quite often it is used badly. When it is used as supremely well as this, suspense is at its ultimate.

9. The Occult

WHERE the supernatural is involved, film technique is equal to the occasion, affording us a near-subliminal glimpse of a ghost or a superimposed impression of some transparent manifestation. In 1912 the going was crude, judging by Cecil Hepworth's one-reel comedy *One Too Exciting Night*, in which a silly ass procured himself a quiet little cottage in the country where he could retreat from the giddy city whirl. A local man, seeing him about to enter the place, pauses at the garden gate with a word of warning. The house is deemed to be haunted and the well-meaning villager declares that personally he would not spend a single night under its roof. With much silent mime, the silly ass conveys his intention to laugh the matter off. He retires to his bed. During the night, however, ornaments in the bedroom begin to shift their positions, and an apparition in a sheet materialises through the window. Save for this last touch, not much is accomplished that could not be managed just as well in the theatre, but in their day the crude technical tricks were probably a wow.

The spooky funfair touch respecting ghosts had been maintained in the cinema over the years. Ludicrous (and concomitantly reassuring) essays in the ghostly sphere are often set in the traditional locales of isolated houses and remote islands. One story of ghosts and zombies on a dark island, reached by row-boat through fog, has served merrily for Bob Hope (in 1940, when it was called *The Ghost Breakers*) and also for Jerry Lewis and Dean Martin (in 1952, with the title changed to *Scared Stiff*; both versions directed by George Marshall). Once they reached the island, there was a sinister castle, of course; and much was made of a disquieting coffin. The tremblings of funny men in the face of the supernatural permit us the luxury of a superior chortle. The big laugh at the end of *The Ghost Breakers*, after things would seem to have been resolved rationally, is Bob Hope's startled awareness that now he is beholding "the real ghost". There is incidental leeway there, despite the guffaw, to accommodate those who are disinclined to shrug off as nonsense any hint of the supernatural.

The others derive pleasure from their shrugs and chortles. This does them a certain amount of good, no doubt. Comedy makes the thing easy: it is not a question of suspending disbelief, but of being able so readily to eliminate believing, since the goings-on are very funny. Laughter is the safety valve, and laughter will be heard on occasion when the supernatural comes into a film that is serious, or at any rate straight-faced. The instinct to eliminate believing is born of a deeper, possibly sub-conscious, inclination to believe. Bela Lugosi, making a curtain speech after a stage performance of *Dracula*, wagged an admonitory finger at the audience and said, "Don't forget there *are* such things"; and then he vanished in a great puff of smoke, accompanied by a mild explosion. This sent everybody out into the dark night in high glee, and probably diminished the likelihood of ensuing nightmares. The parody had been comforting.

Playing upon the imagination and the sensibility of the spectator, the wise dealer in supernatural suspense will be aware that grounds for disbelief are vague. One wants to disbelieve for safety's sake; therefore one laughs to reassure oneself. There is a parallel with the compulsive beholder of a street accident, who neither steps forward to help nor walks away because he cannot be of any help, but simply stands and ogles, not necessarily on account of sensation-lust but more probably because he has been immobilized by the thought "Thank God it isn't me." Seeing a person on the screen terrified by a ghost, that subconscious reaction is even stronger, so he laughs it away.

This understandable tendency makes the going hard for a director in a case like Robert Florey's *The Beast With Five Fingers* (1946). The film is a straight-faced melodrama, in which Hilary Cummins (Peter Lorre) is pursued by a severed but evidently living hand which scampers about a brooding house. Sometimes the technical trickery is obvious enough, as when the wrist is emerging from conveniently deep shadow. Elsewhere the mechanics are remarkable. The hand plays a piano. Cummins shuts it away in a drawer but it clambers out. Eventually, it climbs up his chest toward his throat and strangles him. Credibly enough, the mounting hysteria of Cummins is not dissimilar to the jitters of the haunted comedians. So one laughs, especially at the desperate measures taken by Cummins in his panic: he nails the hand down, he locks it in a safe, all to no avail.

A supernatural visitation might possibly be on the benign side: when Death chooses to mingle with mortals for three days, in the guise of one Prince Sirki (Fredric March: *Death Takes a Holiday*, 1933, directed by Mitchell Leisen), nobody in the world dies during this period; but then on the other hand the heroine forsakes her mortal fiancé for love of the prince, who wraps his cloak around her at fadeout time. There is also the contrite ghost (Noël Coward) in *The Scoundrel* (1935, directed by Ben Hecht and Charles MacArthur), a libertine who is dead but has been granted one more month on earth in mortal form, in order to find somebody willing to weep on his behalf and thereby save his soul from perdition.

These are among the occasional exceptions to the cinema's ghostly rule: generally apparitions are malevolent. In one of the ghost stories that comprise *Kwaidan* (1965, directed by Masaki Kobayashi), the broad strokes of Japanese acting combine with neat tricks of cinema to make such manifestations very persuasive. A samurai, Kannai (Ganemon Naka-mura), pauses during a hot day's march to drink some water in the courtyard of a temple. When he dips a cup in the water and raises it toward his mouth, he sees a face reflected up-side-down on the surface of the liquid. He looks about him, nervously, but nobody is there. He throws the liquid away, and refills the cup. The same face appears again on the surface of the water, this time the right way up and sneering. Kannai, both hot and frightened, drinks the water, reflection and all. That night, when he is alone again, the man whose face was reflected enters the room materialising from out of the shadows. The ghost is a nobleman, as his white robe testifies. He sneers again. The bright heat of the sun has given place now to the cool white-walled room where Kannai is on duty, but the panic aroused by the sneering face is equally dis-turbing in this calm environment. Kannai strikes at the nobleman, who vanishes. The following night, Kannai is very ill at ease. At midnight he has visitors, three samurai who say that he has hurt their master, who will return and take his revenge when he has recovered. Kannai attacks the three, but each one of them disappears as Kannai's weapon strikes his body, only to reappear again in another position. Kannai's futile blows, and the abrupt vanishings of each of the three in turn, repeated again and again, swiftly, bring the tormented man to the point of frenzy. Then, suddenly, his weapon seems to penetrate the bodies of each of the three in turn, and each time the picture freezes in a momentarily held image of death. Kannai is exhausted but relieved. He stands outdoors, where dry leaves blow around his feet, and suddenly all three dead samurai reappear, and converge upon him. Exceptional colour photography, and no more than a sufficiency of formalism, give the strange mystery a refinement of terror.

In a style more familiar to us, the ability to foresee things that will happen in the future was the mainspring of a typical melodrama from Hollywood: John Farrow's *Night Has a Thousand Eyes* (1948). Until the concluding phase of the story, the melodrama was muted, and at the same time endowed with a nice modification of the glossy look that can serve cinema melodrama very well if discretion is observed. In-deed, this quality is no small part of the superiority that

Hitchcock's American films have over those of his earlier work in England. The Hollywood efficiency in matters of lighting and visual tone, often carried to such glamorous extremes as to look false and preposterous, can be harnessed by the right hands to tremendous advantage, as evidenced by the best of the westerns (Ford, Sturges, Zinnemann, and McLaglen are directors who come immediately to mind) and by thrillers in which the realism needs to be heightened. By degrees, this Hollywood know-how has been assimilated by British film-makers, for better and for worse according to the subject: generally for worse in anything broaching the "epic", and generally for better in thrillers. John Farrow did yeoman duty in this line during the Hollywood forties. A romantic gloss, night and smoke and railway lines, is indigenous to the initial effect of *Night Has a Thousand Eyes*. At once, as in *The Big Clock*, Farrow has us intrigued by his visual mood-making as much as by the mystery of the given situation. A girl (Gail Russell) is attempting to commit suicide by jumping from a bridge across the railway tracks. Below a train is approaching. In the nick of time she is prevented by the hero (John Lund). He takes her to the station buffet, where a professional fortune-teller (Edward G. Robinson) is waiting. The girl does not seem pleased to see him. They drink coffee, and the fortune-teller talks. What he says is depicted in flashbacks.

This fortune-teller, in his carefree shady days, was a fake, purporting to foretell the future for members of the theatre audience. Then, one night in the middle of his act, something frightening came into his mind. The details were not clear, but there was sufficient for him to single out a couple in the audience and advise them to hurry home. This they did, just in time to prevent their baby from burning to death. From there on, the fortune-teller's life was hell. Ill-equipped to cope with this new-found ability, this ironic intrusion of the "gift" he had been faking, he drew scant consolation from the fact that he could foresee happy things as well as tragic ones. Race-track winners were known to him in advance. Profitable business manœuvres could be undertaken in the confidence of foreknowledge. But he was uncomfortable. One bleak and rainy day, at a stage door before the show, he bought a newspaper from a passing boy, had one of his psychic twinges, and shouted a warning to the retreating boy, bidding him to take care crossing roads.

Almost at once, from offscreen, there comes a horrendous screech of tyres. The death of the boy, like the burning of the baby, has not been depicted directly, either as a flash-forward when the fortune-teller foresees the event or as a visual representation of the event itself. The sensational stuff is being saved for later. The establishing phase is succinct, and reliant to a very great degree upon Edward G. Robinson's splendidly controlled expressions of interior disquiet. A big personality actor, with a big face, he knew how to rein in the histrionics; and with such a face as his the minimal expression in front of the camera was enough to register strongly in the magnified image that would reach the screen.

The film is well advanced by the time this flashback period is over and we are back at the station buffet over the coffee cups. One senses that the coffee is cold and foul. The fortune-teller has predicted terrible things that concern the girl who attempted suicide. Now the plot moves rather ploddingly toward a climax that strains credulity to its limits and beyond. Farrow's preparatory work in the flashbacks has been so shrewd, however, that the enormities to come are more compulsive than they deserve to be. This climax takes place in the girl's residence, an affluent one, overlooking the nightscape of Los Angeles. The fortune-teller has had one of his unclear visions. Their lack of clarity is a good thing, of course, making us more prone to credit what he says and at the same time keeping us mildly curious about how events will measure up to his vague predictions. He says he has foreseen the girl lying dead under the stars; as well as a confusion of other images, like a glass falling and smashing to pieces, and the paws of a lion. Easy enough to have a glass fall and smash: this happens, and suspense is maintained. Then a radio announcement is heard: a lion has escaped from the zoo. In terms of plot construction this is the really fatal touch: the sort of thing that might just possibly happen in real life but should not be permitted to happen at such a time in the course of a film. It is a "red herring"-lion, anyway, and, even if it were not, the very mention of it is death to straight-faced

"World gone awry"—Eddie Constantine in ALPHAVILLE.

suspense and life to the escape-guffaw. The mood is gone, and is not to be recaptured.

One thing is absolutely clear in the fortune-teller's mind. The girl's death will occur at eleven o'clock at night. This hour is fast approaching. In the drawing room, the girl is well attended by friends and police. Through the wide open doors we see the stars, and beneath them a shadowy garden. The stars and the hour are fine suspense factors, if blighted by the loose lion. Now another tiresome touch is introduced. From behind a curtain an arm emerges, and fingers tamper with the minute hand on the clock, putting it forward so that the fatal hour of eleven appears to pass without mishap. Not a soul among those assembled has observed the antiquarian doings: the lurker behind the curtain has presumably gone now to lurk in the garden under the stars. The girl, of course, instead of going off to bed with a glass of hot milk or something, strolls out into the garden on her own. There, on the true stroke of eleven, she is attacked, right beside the stone statue of a lion. Her head rests near its paws. The fortune-teller comes running, convinced that soon she will be dead as he foresaw; but, in his wild attempt to ward off the inevitable, he gets the bullet intended for the girl. The death under the stars is his own. An incidental character is apprehended as the killer.

The escaped lion and the tampering with time are crude examples of valid suspense measures. By relieving tension for the threatened character, such measures increase tension for the spectator. The radio announces eventually that the escaped lion has been caught. The girl probably thinks "So much for all that," but the spectator does not, because he knows that the fortune-teller has predicted many things that have really happened and that somehow or other there must be more than this to his vision of the lion's paws. Then, when the girl heaves a sigh of relief because the hour of eleven has passed, the spectator knows that it has not passed and that when she goes out under the stars there are still a couple of dangerous minutes in hand. The strategy of suspense in such cases does require finesse, however. It doesn't really do to bring in a real lion, even in the radio news; nor does it do to have the murderer put the clock forward, because what the hell does he care whether or not he kills the girl on the stroke of eleven? He took a risk, lurking there behind the curtain. He could have waited until five past eleven, always assuming that the silly girl would go out alone into the garden, a matter over which the murderer had no control. He could have killed her under the stars beside the stone lion at 11.07 or in the first light of dawn by the tum-tum tree. But no: it is he, the murderer, at considerable inconvenience to himself, who must force these elements of the fortune-teller's predictions to come true.

I recount this climax, and all that is wrong about it, in some detail because it intrigues me, containing as it does good basic principles of suspense-building that have been spoiled by rough-hewn contrivances. The escape-laugh gives place to the

115

smile of bland derision. But the build-up in the earlier part is superb of its kind, and Robinson's acting, even under the stars, is a pleasure to note.

Earlier in the same decade, Robinson had a more interesting brush with the occult in a solemn version of Oscar Wilde's black joke, *Lord Arthur Savile's Crime*. This was one of the three short stories that were related in *Flesh and Fantasy* (1943), directed by Julien Duvivier during his Hollywood sojourn. For obvious reasons, Lord Arthur was re-thought as an American solicitor working in London, and renamed Marshall Tyler (Robinson). The plot was virtually the same as Wilde's but straight-faced instead of satirical. What might have been high comedy became elevated melodrama.

At a party, a reader of palms named Podger (Thomas Mitchell) has been engaged to entertain the guests. Tyler takes a cynical view of fortune-telling, but Podger unsettles him by apparently foreseeing something terrible in his palm. Reluctant to dampen the party, Podger does not disclose his premonition until Tyler seeks him out privately and demands to know. Then Podger tells him that his palm marks him out as a murderer. This worries Tyler to such an extent that he thinks it best to break off his romantic attachment to Rowena (Anna Lee). He tells her that the date of their marriage must be postponed. Tyler's one desire now is to commit a murder and be done with it. With poison he endeavours to despatch one Lady Pamela Hardwick (Dame May Whitty), and, when that doesn't work, he tries to kill the Dean of Norwalk (C. Aubrey Smith), also without success. By now beside himself, he is walking on London Bridge at night when he encounters Podger and, with what might be construed as poetic justice, strangles him. The police turn up. Tyler runs away, dashing through ground occupied by a circus, where he is run over and killed by a truck. This incident is observed by a tight-rope walker (Charles Boyer) and the film slips smoothly into its next story, wherein this observer is plagued by a dream in which he falls from the tightrope in the middle of his act.

Given such a yarn, it would have been much better to stick to Wilde's mood and to have a film not unlike Robert Hamer's stylish essay in extravagance, *Kind Hearts and*

Coronets (1949). Wilde's short story has Lord Arthur pitching the fortune-teller into the water; and when a passing policeman inquires if he has dropped something, Lord Arthur merely replies, "Nothing of importance," and goes on his way. The tale is equally trenchant as a study in obsession when expressed in terms of high comedy. It would have been *de rigueur* for Duvivier's version to bring the murderer to a grim end rather than leave him free, so the transformation from comedy into melodrama was undoubtedly an aid in this respect, although, as *Kind Hearts and Coronets* proved, it is quite possible to manage this operation in a witty style. More probably the motivation was to give the three varied stories in the Duvivier film a certain seriousness in common. Each of them has a well-judged appreciation of the shifty terrain where fantasy and reality (i.e., flesh) begin to merge. The efficiency-glamour of the Hollywood look is assimilated by Duvivier in *Flesh and Fantasy*, and is apt enough. The initial party scene and the confrontations of Robinson and Thomas Mitchell are ham most delicately sliced. And although the attempted murders that fail are inevitably risky, since the black humour of the concept will cling to them no matter how serious everybody tries to be, the darker strain is palpable and the ultimate murder on the bridge works very well in the melodramatic manner. The entire episode suggests that fantasy can be interpreted as an extension of human frailty.

10. Fantasy and Reality

THE borderline that lies between fantasy and reality is often ill-defined, in the cinema as in life. Andrew L. Stone's *Cry Terror!* (1957) lives up to its exclamation mark with a welter of sensational incident: a high-tension thriller that strains credulity, yet any given part of it might be defended as realistic. Not least the situation of a woman (Inger Stevens) who needs desperately to reach a vital destination but discovers that she is driving her car in the very opposite direction on a motorway that permits no turning for miles. Reality and nightmare are one. The parody-thriller will make game of this, as in Leslie Martinson's *Fathom* (1967), when heroine and equivocal hero exchange dialogue essential to the plot while at the same time they are on the run from a furious bull in a sunlit bullring. Conveniently, the lining of the hero's jacket is red and he has the chance to play toreador. In both cases, the locations are genuine.

For science-fiction, a studio mock-up has often served; but, to substantiate its claim of being "only one step ahead of present reality", *Robinson Crusoe on Mars* (1964, directed by Byron Haskin) needed a location that would seem as credible as the scientific details of its plot. A vast and forbidding territory, eloquently apt, was near enough to hand: Death Valley, California. Here an astronaut (Paul Mantee), who has survived collision with a meteor, prowls the craggy landscape in search of the capsule that held his co-pilot, finds it wrecked and the hand of the dead co-pilot lying in the gravel beside it. At the hint of a movement behind a rock, he draws his gun, but discovers that a monkey, space-suited like himself, and along for experimental purposes, has also survived to share with him four months of suspenseful solitude. During this time (and for at least half of the film's length) the only words

118

that are spoken, save for an occasional remark to the monkey, are messages for posterity which the astronaut records. "A guy can lick the problems of heat, water, shelter, food. I know. I've done it. But here's the hairiest problem of all. Isolation. Being alone." The screenplay by Ib Melchior and John Higgins maintains a bemusing parallel to the story of Defoe's Robinson Crusoe, with the added irony of scientific man fighting for survival like a primitive. The air on Mars is thin. His oxygen supply is running out. He finds yellow rocks that can be burned "like coal". Heat sets free the "built-in oxygen", which can be breathed. Also, there are dreams: the dead co-pilot (Adam West) makes a ghostly re-appearance, and the man who has been denied conversation for four months begs him to speak, but there is no reply. There is to be a Friday, however, a slave who has escaped and is pursued by interplanetary villains, attacking in force for the climax.

A lone man will sometimes pit himself against overbearing forces of evil in the cause of freedom. This recurrent suspense gambit is imaginatively extended in Jean-Luc Godard's *Alphaville* (1965). Secret agent Lemmy Caution (Eddie Constantine) has been sent from the outer countries to a space-city of the future named Alphaville, with orders to arrest, or if necessary kill, a professor who has invented the omniscient computer that rules the lives of the citizens. Strongly flavoured with science fiction and comic strip allusions, and winding up with an escape-chase in which cars skid in the snow and several times the visuals are shown in negative, the nightmare provokes laughter that alienates the spectator sufficiently from the emotional norm. It is a disorientating process that not only leaves the mind cool to contemplate the cautionary message (the hero's name, already familiar to French filmgoers in lightweight movies, proves very apt in *Alphaville*), but also suggests a world gone awry. Fantasy and absurdity jostle close to life. The city itself is really Paris, photographed by Raoul Coutard in such a way as to make it look chill and forbidding: geometrical and glassy buildings, grey or fog-mantled exteriors, and claustrophobic corridors are forever reminding us that Alphaville, for all its strangeness, has an affinity with the world we inhabit now. The dominating computer, reducing life to "logic", eroding

119

humanity, replacing the individual will to think and act with a tranquillised submission to specific "rules", is a menace so much more frightening than Frankenstein's monster that the spectator cannot be expected to assess its threat rationally if he is emotionally involved.

In a way, a computer is an easy target. The instinctive reaction of many is to jeer whenever a present-day computer "makes mistakes", because the computer is potentially capable of doing work previously done by a quantity of human beings, and consequently seems likely to cause unemployment. This is a political problem, boring and depressing but demanding attention. Deeper, in the imponderable future, is the danger of human readiness to submit. This easy antidote to the perplexed mind can be seen looming around in the twentieth century. The pace has been hot, so the natural desire is to cool down, and to let others do the thinking and make the decisions. Thus, the suspense in *Alphaville*, incorporating the entertainment elements (rescue of the professor's beautiful daughter, and climactic escape-chase), is a lingering suspense: an exhortation to resist the luxury of non-thinking, lest technology in the wrong hands should reach the point where machines are the masters of men. It is an old thriller (and for that matter comedy) motif, which has become increasingly meaningful with the passage of time.

In Alphaville, by computer's decree, killing is a spectator sport. At a swimming pool, illogical men (that is to say men who have been using their individual minds instead of obeying the regulations) are blindfolded and made to stand on the diving boards. They are shot and fall into the water, whereupon girls with knives dive into the pool and hack at the bodies. All this is greeted with polite applause from the tranquillised onlookers. The atmosphere is totally unemotional.

The killer instinct is organised provocatively in another future-world, that of Elio Petri's *La decima vittima* (*The 10th Victim*, 1965). The period is A.D. 2000. War has been forbidden, and those who need an outlet for their native aggression can participate officially in "The Hunt". There is no need for them to lurk on remote islands like Zaroff (see Chapter 4). Should the citizen in a city street observe two running men, or even a running man and woman, firing guns at one another, no notice is taken: it is official, they are members of the hunt, and the killer will receive money as a prize when he completes the job. Death by bullets fired from a brassière, or by catapulting the victim from a poolside chair into the water where a crocodile is waiting (a ruse that fails, but is demonstrated for our edification), are but two of the methods used by ingenious members of the hunt, and there are foregatherings at such joints as the Club Masoch to enliven the scene. Although the vein is that of strenuous low comedy with one slippery foot in the field of sophistication, this singular jape does throw up the question of whether the world can arrive at a workable solution to the problem of the aggressive instinct.

Fantasy comes closer still to reality in John Frankenheimer's *Seconds* (1966), from a novel by David Ely. The urge to escape from routine is the spur for Hamilton (John Randolph), a middle-aged American who is well-to-do but markedly debilitated by social conformity. His solid existence seems far removed from the aspirations of his college days, and this depresses him. After some sweaty hesitation, he pays an undercover organisation to reconstitute him scientifically. The world is to be informed that he is dead, an assertion that will be backed up by somebody else's disfigured corpse: thus Hamilton becomes "Wilson" (Rock Hudson), "a reborn". Unfortunately, in his new life, he proves to be one of the organisation's not infrequent failures. As an affluent quasi-bohemian he discovers that he is subject to the same kind of social confinement that distressed him as Hamilton. Consequently, and more than somewhat peremptorily, the organisation kills him off: his disfigured corpse will serve another hopeful applicant for "rebirth".

Aided by the veteran camera stylist James Wong Howe, Frankenheimer goes at all this with a pertinent but monotonously persistent flow of distorted images. Initially this works very well. The opening shot is a distant overhead view of people bustling through the concourse of a large railway station: figures in a nerve-ridden landscape. From this the eye is jolted to a close shot of one individual in the crowd, a man who follows Hamilton as he makes his way toward a platform. The distorting lens follows the legs of this man: the

121

legs are elongated, curved, moving rapidly. The light is dim, and, in the hurry of catching the train, Hamilton does not get a good look at the man, who hands him a scrap of paper just as the train departs. Hamilton looks at the address written on the paper and sweats; then he moves on into a carriage of the train, which seems tunnel-like, stretching away from him and overburdened with weary humans like himself. He finds a seat, tries to do a crossword, and then looks again at the scrap of paper. Eerie music has started up.

At his destination, his wife is waiting as usual to drive him home. She talks as she drives, about conventional things which would appear to be going conventionally well, but the curve of the windscreen is reflecting the landscape ahead and this reflected area to the left of the frame is continually moving "against" the couple in the car, suggesting that their progress in life is relentlessly opposed.

In his study that night, Hamilton awaits a 'phone call: a follow-up, we gather, to one he has received the night before. He is edgy: the room is deep in shadow, his face picked out sharply by the light from his desk lamp. The 'phone rings, uncommonly loudly: more than once Frankenheimer heightens sounds as well as visuals. The ensuing telephone conversation, with one Charlie whom Hamilton had thought to be dead long since, is enigmatic. Thriller-fashion, information is withheld. This is a mistake, in my opinion (the novel does the same thing): there is no reason why the spectator should not know at least as much as Hamilton knows, since he is the character we are meant to be concerned about and suspense is keen enough without forcing a mystery that cannot be maintained. In any case an immediate statement by Charlie's voice, specifying that rebirth is being offered, would have increased the rather superior pathos of the following bedroom scene, where Hamilton's wife asks what is troubling him and gets no answer. In moderate long-shot, the bedroom has a yawning, hollow look to it: in close-up, Hamilton's face on the pillow is fearful, and he sweats.

He continues to sweat at noon next day, in a glassy impersonal office at the bank where he works (and is next in line for presidency). Mouth awry, he dictates a routine letter, compounded of jargon, rejecting a plea for financial aid.

Then he is off to the given address, which proves to be incorrect: no doubt a precautionary measure on the part of the undercover organisation, but another unnecessary delay for the spectator. However, the false address is moody: it is a dry-cleaning establishment where a sinewy man operates the trouser-press, his forearm elongated and curved grotesquely as he reaches toward the foreground of the frame. From here, Hamilton is directed to a meat depot: a sharp cut now, to a line of carcasses on hooks, moving on overhead rails. Hamilton is led through macabre corridors of carcasses, and, in a darker part of the same place, two such carcasses are being shifted, but these are wrapped in cheesecloth and might conceivably be the dead bodies of humans. Now, in a van of the "High-Pro Meat Packing Co.", Hamilton is driven to an anonymous office building, where at last the spectator is enlightened about the nature of the plot.

When at length the plastic surgery is performed the technique of the film is at its best. The sequence begins with a fairly close shot of the surgeon's hand drawing a line on some section of Hamilton's anatomy. Ensuing shots are quick and clinical, stressing details of the face. These are followed by a splendid little scene between the reborn "Wilson" and the surgeon. The transition of actors is quite neat. Wilson is not Hamilton in appearance, but Rock Hudson's head is wrapped in a bandage for the time being, with slits for eyes and mouth. He cannot speak. Instead he utters animal moans. "Don't do that," says the surgeon rather sharply. He is an edgy man, understandably, but he adopts a bedside tone almost at once, and tells Wilson that his teeth have been removed and his larynx treated to effect a change of voice. He adds that the virility that comes with the operation will be that of a bull.

The removal of the head bandage takes place with Wilson's back to the camera. The hair is still the hair of Hamilton, but the neck is more youthful and firm. The camera pans across to a mirror with side panels, and in triplicate we see the reborn, stitches very evident on his face and deep shadows, possibly bruises, beneath his eyes. The eyes themselves are bright with tears. This is one of the occasional passages where distort lensing is suspended: without it, the impact of the triple reflection is very strong.

The face is seen to improve gradually, but in a short amount of screen time, and Hamilton is transported to California. He is to pose as a painter, in a house at Malibu beach with a manservant provided by the organisation. At first there is no distortion of images at the house, but it has a strangeness of its own and a subtle strangeness at that, partly on account of the quiet contrast to what has gone before and partly because of its whiteness and the diffused sunlight through the big windows and the solitary expanse of beach outside. There is more eerie music. Another series of fairly quick cuts: Wilson's inadequate attempts to master the chosen art, alternating with morose wandering along the sand. There is a delicate hint of a possible blessing in his encounter with a blonde on the beach. Her name is Norma (Salome Jens). She is dressed in black, Wilson in white: and there on the desolate beach a tenuous rapport begins, not exactly spiritual, not exactly sexy: Norma turns out to be a pawn of the organisation, there to be of help but a potential source of danger to Wilson if her help should prove inadequate.

When Norma takes Wilson to Santa Barbara for grape-harvesting festivities, the ensuing middle-aged hippie-scamper begins like a happening that just happened to be photographed by a nimble-footed cameraman. A procession weaves in drab jubilation toward the grapes, and eventually the least inhibited plunge raw into an outsize vat and slosh around in the juice. Norma goes in, to Wilson's embarrassment, but soon he is peeled and persuaded as well and, to the strains of "What Shall We Do With A Drunken Sailor?", he responds to the experience with a beaming smile, while the camerawork indulges in some spasmodic romantic misting and glints of light. This is the key moral scene of the film. It is the only occasion on which Wilson looks happy: but his is a far-gone happiness, and the mood of the entire caper is that of desperation . . . sensual pleasure reaching urgently toward unrealism.

Unhappily the Malibu phase of the film is trapped too firmly between the strong suspense of the opening sequences, protracted though they be, and the high-pressure tactics of what is to follow. As a result, Wilson's stab at life as a reborn seems to be skimped. It is a question of balance. The grape harvest episode goes a long way toward redressing the balance. It has a stylistic quality of its own to set against the potent distort-phases. Yet the entire Malibu phase is lacking in substance. Save for the scene in the vat, there is no moment when Wilson seems even remotely likely to succeed as a re-born. The moral tone is dour and inevitable. Therefore the suspense that follows smacks of too much contrivance, an impression augmented by the heavy return of distort-lensing.

The organisation itself is anxious for each of its reborns to be a success, and yet the incidence of bungling by its em-ployees is notable. The psychologist who thought Wilson ought to adopt the life of a painter, the freedom-ridden Norma, and the manservant John are inept. John suggests repeatedly that Wilson should give a cocktail party for his Malibu neighbours. I should have thought a little series of quiet dinner parties would have been more appropriate: one neighbour at a time, with his wife or mistress, if any, and perhaps Norma as well to ease the conversation along after her fashion. But no: into the house troops a whole herd of neighbours, and, having saddled Wilson with them, John is too incompetent to prevent his master from drinking to excess. Upon this cue, the distorted images and perspectives return with a rush. Wilson begins prattling about his former life as Hamilton to a plump intoxicated blonde, who seems unlikely to assimilate the significance of what he says, and all the men at the party converge upon the host. There are quick shots of individual faces, all menacing. Wilson is carried Hamlet-wise to his room and dumped on the bed. The camera gives us his subjective view, with an apt wobble, of the threatening circle of men looming over him. John breaks through them, loosens Wilson's tie, and tells him that these men are reborns like himself. He should have said that sooner, way back when he was making up the guest list: the calamity is forced upon Wilson, so that the "stay-in-your-own-backyard" moral can be rammed home hard. Wilson screams for Norma, who speaks to him more sharply than the surgeon did before: this is Wilson's first intimation that Norma's rapport was part of the organisation's service.

125

There is a long close-up of Wilson's face on the bed, sobbing: this is very good, as indeed are most of the visuals in themselves, as distinct from the accumulated effect of their intensity which grows unnecessarily harrowing.

Later, lying inert and alone, Wilson picks up the 'phone when it rings. Charlie's voice urges him to stay and make another effort to succeed; but before Charlie's plea is over, Frankenheimer has already cut, admirably, to the next shot, showing Wilson at the airport making his getaway. The camera travels with him along a glass-walled corridor. Beyond the glass, which bars their way, the other reborns of the colony are racing in futile pursuit.

Wilson returns to the home he had as Hamilton. It is peaceful and quiet, and during his visit the visual distortion is suspended again. The maid who admits him is seen hazily through fly-proof netting of the outer door, which opens like a veil being lifted on the past. For a short, quiet time he is alone in the room that used to be his study. On the mantel is a photograph of his former self: he picks it up. Hamilton's "widow" comes in. He tells her he knew her late husband and would like a memento of him. She accepts this with only minor surprise. Wilson gathers that Hamilton is not much missed. Mrs. Hamilton, the total suburban conformist, is reconciled to living her own orderly life. Wilson leaves carrying an athletic trophy from the ambitious college days: as he walks away from the house there is a soundtrack overlay of Mrs. Hamilton's voice explaining that this is the best thing she can find by way of a memento. A car is parked by the sidewalk. The manservant John is there, waiting. Wilson says that now he wants to go back, and John agrees cryptically that he shall. He is not going back to Malibu, however, but to the organisation's headquarters. Wilson sits in the moving car, holding the trophy that symbolises youthful virility and dreams.

After more menace at the headquarters, Wilson listens to a salutary little homily from the head man, who is benign in manner and, significantly, very old. He tells Wilson how his own dream of giving men a second chance at life has become increasingly difficult to realise.

As Wilson, strapped down, is wheeled to the operating

theatre to be killed, distorted images abound. Walls of corridors curve and swirl. Wilson screams, and is gagged. Before the act of elimination, the surgeon expresses regret, because he has to undo what he considers to be one of his most satisfactory physical transformations. Subjective shot: a strong light burns down on Wilson, the surgeon's hand advances holding an instrument and moves downward to the foot of the frame. As it reaches Wilson's head, the noise it makes is harsh.

The technique of *Seconds*, if ponderous as a whole, is full of intelligent detail. The major flaws are in the marshalling of material: and especially in the seeming inadequacy of the chance Wilson is given to make a go of things at Malibu. The strongly implicit conjuration to adjust to reality instead of pursuing elusive ideals was capable of a modification that would have made the film less depressing and possibly helpful. The human wish to begin again is a dream that can be harnessed. A hope of recapturing an idealistic past sustains the heroine of Jacques Demy's *Lola* (1961), although the film is constructed in such a way as to indicate, subtly, that the romantic fulfilment of the dream will not necessarily last into an infinite future: what it will do is make that future more tolerable. Humans are imperfect creatures, unrealistically striving toward perfection, fortified by their dreams.

The wakeful, wishful dreams begin in childhood, to counteract the darker dreams that come unbidden in the night with their cautionary and lasting terrors. Humans remain susceptible to them throughout life, and the suspense film is often based upon the nightmares of the innocent. The fear of the unknown and the urge to maintain illusion will find occasional expression in a film that has a child as its central character. "We've got to think of lies, and tell them all the time, and then they won't find out the truth," declares twelve-year-old Felipe (Bobby Henrey) in *The Fallen Idol* (1948, directed by Carol Reed; screenplay by Graham Greene). Believing in tall tales that have been told him by the butler Baines (Ralph Richardson), Felipe invents lies to protect the butler who is suspected, wrongly, of having murdered his wife. Felipe, who has been menaced by the wife, and conditioned to think of Baines as the heroic avenger, manufactures fantasies when

127

questioned by the police and thereby makes the case against the butler stronger than ever. The instinct toward fantasy is still more potent in the *Chickamauga* episode of Robert Enrico's *Au cœur de la vie* (1963), a film made up of three stories of the American civil war by Ambrose Bierce. *Chickamauga* is a visually poetic and at the same time frightening account of a small boy who happens by chance upon a scene of death in a forest. A battle has been fought. Many soldiers, dead or dying, lie in ghostly testament to mortality and inhumanity. The child does not understand: a strange other-worldliness absorbs him as he moves among the bodies, observes the martial drum, and indulges in a little soldier game of his own. There is, for the adult spectator, a muted terror, a sense of foreboding. When the child is done with his game and heads for home, he finds his parents dead and the house in ruins.

So the suspense brought on by life begins quite early. It begins in unawareness, but awareness soon grows. Then doubt and uncertainty and the urge to know and the dread of knowing become a part of living, to be checked or assimilated, or, if only tentatively, sublimated. As an aid to sublimation, suspense in the cinema, vicarious but meaningful, serious or comic, has a purpose to serve.

Books Consulted

CAHN, WILLIAM: *Harold Lloyd's World of Comedy* (George Allen and Unwin Ltd., London).

KNIGHT, ARTHUR: *The Liveliest Art. A Panoramic History of the Movies* (The Macmillan Company, New York).

LANCHESTER, ELSA: *Charles Laughton and I* (Faber and Faber, London).

STEPHENSON, RALPH, and DEBRIX, J. R.: *The Cinema as Art* (Penguin Books, London).

Wolfenstein, Martha, and Leites, Nathan: *Movies: a psychological study* (The Free Press, Glencoe, Illinois).

Wood, Robin: *Hitchcock's films* (A. Zwemmer Ltd., London/ A. S. Barnes & Co., New York).

The screenplay of Astruc's *Le puits et le pendule* is published in *L'Avant-Scène*, November, 1966.

Filmography

ALPHAVILLE (1965). *Dir. and sc.:* Jean-Luc Godard. *ph.:* Raoul Coutard. *mus.:* Paul Misraki. *ed.:* Agnès Guillemot. *players:* Eddie Constantine, Anna Karina, Akim Tamiroff, Howard Vernon, Laszlo Szabo.

ASCENSEUR POUR L'ÉCHAFAUD (LIFT TO THE SCAFFOLD) (1957). *Dir.:* Louis Malle. *sc.:* Malle and Roger Nimier. From the novel by Noël Calef. *ph.:* Henri Decaë. *mus.:* Miles Davis. *des.:* Rino Mondellini and Jean Mandaroux. *players:* Maurice Ronet, Jeanne Moreau, Lino Ventura, Georges Poujouly, Yori Bertin.

AU CŒUR DE LA VIE (1963). *Dir. and sc.:* Robert Enrico. Based on three stories by Ambrose Bierce. *ph.:* Jean Boffety. *mus.:* Henri Lanoé. *des.:* Frédéric de Pascale. *players:* Le petit Pilou, Edwin Moatti, Stéphane Fey, François and Eric Frankiel, Frédérique Ruchaud, Roger Jacquet, Anne Cornaly. The first completed section of this film was initially shown by itself under the title *La Rivière du Hibou* (*Incident at Owl Creek*) in 1961.

AUSSI LONGUE ABSENCE, UNE (1961). *Dir.:* Henri Colpi in collaboration with Jasmine Chasney. *sc.:* Marguerite Duras and Gérard Jarlot. *ph.:* Marcel Weiss. *mus.:* Georges Delerue. *des.:* Maurice Colasson. *ed.:* Jasmine

Chasney. *players:* Alida Valli, Georges Wilson, Jacques Harden, Amédée, Catherine Fontenay, Diana Lepvrier.

BEAST WITH FIVE FINGERS, THE (1946). *Prod.:* William Jacobs. *Dir.:* Robert Florey. *sc.:* Curt Siodmak. From the story by William Fryer Harvey. *ph.:* Wesley Anderson. *mus.:* Max Steiner. *ed.:* Frank Magee. *players:* Robert Alda, Andrea King, Peter Lorre, Victor Francen, J. Carrol Naish, Charles Dingle.

BIG CLOCK, THE (1947). *Prod.:* Richard Maibaum. *Dir.:* John Farrow. *sc.:* Jonathan Latimer. Story by Kenneth Fearing. *ph.:* John Seitz. *mus.:* Victor Young. *des.:* Hans Dreier, Roland Anderson, Albert Mazaki. *ed.:* Eda Warren. *players:* Ray Milland, Charles Laughton, Maureen O'Sullivan, George Macready, Rita Johnson, Elsa Lanchester.

BLACKMAIL (1929). *Dir.:* Alfred Hitchcock. *sc.:* Hitchcock, Benn W. Levy, Charles Bennett. From a play by Bennett. *ph.:* John Cox. *mus.:* Hubert Bath, Henry Stafford. *des.:* Norman Arnold, Wilfred Arnold. *ed.:* Emile de Ruelle. *players:* Anny Ondra, John Longden, Sara Allgood, Charles Paton, Donald Calthrop, Cyril Ritchard.

BLOW-UP (1966). *Prod.:* Carlo Ponti. *Dir.:* Michelangelo Antonioni. *sc.:* Antonioni, Tonino Guerra. *Eng. dialog.:* Edward Bond. Based on a short story by Julio Cortazar. *ph.:* Carlo Di Palma. Eastmancolor. *mus.:* Herbert Hancock. *des.:* Assheton Gorton. *ed.:* Frank Clarke. *players:* David Hemmings, Vanessa Redgrave, Peter Bowles, Sarah Miles.

BONNES FEMMES, LES (1960). *Prod.:* Robert and Raymond Hakim. *Dir.:* Claude Chabrol. *sc.:* Paul Gégauff. *ph.:* Henri Decaë. *players:* Bernadette Lafont, Lucile Saint Simon, Clothilde Joano, Stéphane Audran, Mario David, A. Ninchi, Jean-Louis Maury, Dinan, Sacha Briquet.

COLLECTOR, THE (1965). *Prod.:* Jud Kinberg, John Kohn. *Dir.:* William Wyler. *sc.:* Stanley Mann, John Kohn. Based on the novel by John Fowles. *ph.:* Robert L.

Surtees, Robert Krasker. Technicolor. *mus.:* Maurice Jarre. *des.:* John Stoll. *ed.:* Robert Swink, David Hawkins. *players:* Terence Stamp, Samantha Eggar, Mona Washbourne, Maurice Dallimore.

CONDAMNÉ À MORT S'EST ÉCHAPPÉ, UN (1956). *Dir. and sc.:* Robert Bresson. Adapted from the book by André Devigny. *ph.:* L. H. Burel. *mus.:* Mass in C minor: Mozart. *players:* François Leterrier, Charles Leclainche, Maurice Beerblock, Roland Monod, Jacques Ertaud, Jean-Paul Delhumeau, Roger Treherne.

CRY TERROR! (1957). *Prod.:* Virginia and Andrew Stone. *Dir. and sc.:* Andrew L. Stone. *ph.:* Walter Strenge. *mus.:* Howard Jackson. *ed.:* Virginia Stone. *players:* James Mason, Rod Steiger, Inger Stevens, Neville Brand, Angie Dickinson.

CUL-DE-SAC (1966). *Prod.:* Gene Gutowski. *Dir.:* Roman Polanski. *sc.:* Polanski and Gerard Brach. *ph.:* Gilbert Taylor. *des.:* Voytek. *ed.:* Alastair McIntyre. *players:* Donald Pleasence, Françoise Dorléac, Lionel Stander, Jack MacGowran, William Franklyn.

DEATH TAKES A HOLIDAY (1933). *Dir.:* Mitchell Leisen. *sc.:* Maxwell Anderson, Gladys Lehman. From a play by Alberto Casella. *players:* Fredric March, Evelyn Venable.

DECIMA VITTIMA, LA (THE 10th VICTIM) (1965). *Prod.:* Carlo Ponti. *Dir.:* Elio Petri. *sc.:* Tonino Guerra, Giorgio Salvioni, Ennio Flaiano, Petri. From a story by Robert Sheckley. *ph.:* Gianno Di Venanzo. Technicolor. *mus.:* Piero Piccioni. *des.:* Giulio Coltellacci. *ed.:* Ruggero Mastroianni. *players:* Marcello Mastroianni, Ursula Andress, Elsa Martinelli, Massimo Serato, Salvo Randone.

DEUXIÈME SOUFFLE, LE (SECOND BREATH) (1966) *Prod.:* Charles Lumbroso, André Labay. *Dir. and sc.:* Jean-Pierre Melville. Based on the novel by José Giovanni. *ph.:* Marcel Combes. *mus.:* Bernard Gérard. *des.:* Jean-Jacques Fabre. *ed.:* Michel Bohème. *players:* Lino Ventura, Paul Meurisse, Raymond Pellegrin, Christine Fabrega, Pierre Zimmer, Michel Constantin, Marcel Bozzufi, Paul Frankeur, Denis Manuel.

131

DR. NO (1962). *Prod.:* Harry Saltzman, Albert R. Broccoli. *Dir.:* Terence Young. *sc.:* Richard Maibaum, Johanna Harwood, Berkely Mather. *ph.:* Ted Moore. Technicolor. *des.:* Ken Adam. *mus.:* Monty Norman. James Bond theme played by the John Barry Orchestra. *ed.:* Peter Hunt. From the novel by Ian Fleming. *players:* Sean Connery, Ursula Andress, Joseph Wiseman, Jack Lord, Bernard Lee, John Kitzmiller.

ESPIONS, LES (1957). *Dir. and sc.:* Henri-Georges Clouzot. From a novel by Egon Hostovsky. *ph.:* Christian Matras. *mus.:* Georges Auric. *des.:* René Renoux. *players:* Martita Hunt, Véra Clouzot, Gabrielle Dorziat, Curt Jurgens, Peter Ustinov, Sam Jaffe, Gérard Sety, O. E. Hasse, Sacha Pitoëff.

EXPERIMENT IN TERROR (GRIP OF FEAR) (1962). *Prod. and dir.:* Blake Edwards. *sc.:* The Gordons, from their novel *Operation Terror*. *ph.:* Philip Lathrop. *mus.:* Henry Mancini. *des.:* Robert Peterson. *ed.:* Patrick McCormack. *players:* Glenn Ford, Lee Remick, Stefanie Powers, Roy Poole, Ned Glass, Anita Loo, Patricia Huston, James Lanphier, Ross Martin.

FALLEN IDOL, THE (1948). *Prod. and Dir.:* Carol Reed. *sc.:* Graham Greene, from his own short story. *ph.:* Georges Périnal. *mus.:* William Alwyn. *des.:* Vincent Korda, James Sawyer. *ed.:* Oswald Hafenrichter. *players:* Ralph Richardson, Michèle Morgan, Sonia Dresdel, Denis O'Dea, Jack Hawkins, Dora Bryan, Bernard Lee, Bobby Henrey.

FATHOM (1967). *Prod.:* John Kohn. *Dir.:* Leslie Martinson. *sc.:* Lorenzo Semple Jr. Based on the novel by Larry Forrester. *ph.:* Douglas Slocombe. DeLuxe colour. Parachute sequences devised by Ken Vos and photographed by Jacques Duborg. *mus.:* John Dankworth. *des.:* Maurice Carter. *ed.:* Max Benedict. *players:* Tony Franciosa, Raquel Welch, Ronald Fraser, Greta Chi, Richard Briers, Tom Adams, Clive Revill.

FLESH AND FANTASY (1943). *Dir.:* Julien Duvivier. *sc.:* Ernest Pascal, Samuel Hoffenstein, Ellis St. Joseph. Based on stories by Oscar Wilde, Laslo Vadnay, Ellis St.

Joseph. *ph.:* Paul Ivano, Stanley Cortez. *players:* Robert Benchley, Betty Field, Robert Cummings, Edward G. Robinson, Thomas Mitchell, Anna Lee, Dame May Whitty, C. Aubrey Smith, Charles Boyer, Barbara Stanwyck.

GHOST BREAKERS, THE (1940). See note under *Scared Stiff.*

L'HOMME DE RIO (THAT MAN FROM RIO) (1964). *Prod.:* Alexandre Mnouchkine, Georges Dancigers. *Dir.:* Philippe de Broca. *sc.:* J. P. Rappeneau, Ariane Mnouchkine, Daniel Boulanger, de Broca. *ph.:* Edmond Séchan. Eastmancolor. *mus.:* Georges Delerue. *players:* Jean-Paul Belmondo, Françoise Dorléac, Jean Servais, Simone Renant, Milton Ribeiro, Ubiraçy de Oliveira, Adolfo Celi.

HOUND OF THE BASKERVILLES, THE (1939). *Prod.:* Darryl F. Zanuck. *Dir.:* Sidney Lanfield. *sc.:* Ernest Pascal. Based on the novel by Sir Arthur Conan Doyle. *ph.:* Peverell Marley. *mus.:* Cyril J. Mockridge. *des.:* Richard Day, Hans Peters. *ed.:* Robert Simpson. *players:* Richard Greene, Basil Rathbone, Nigel Bruce, Wendy Barrie, Lionel Atwill, John Carradine, Morton Lowry, Beryl Mercer.

HUSH, HUSH, SWEET CHARLOTTE (1964). *Prod. and Dir.:* Robert Aldrich. *sc.:* Henry Farrell, Lukas Keller. From a story by Henry Farrell. *ph.:* Joseph Biroc. *mus.:* Frank De Vol. *des.:* William Glasgow. *ed.:* Michael Luciano. *players:* Bette Davis, Olivia de Havilland, Joseph Cotten, Agnes Moorehead, Cecil Kellaway, Victor Buono, Mary Astor.

IN A LONELY PLACE (1950). *Prod.:* Robert Lord. *Dir.:* Nicholas Ray. *sc.:* Andrew Solt. Adaptation by Edmund H. North. Based on a story by Dorothy B. Hughes. *ph.:* Burnett Guffey. *mus.:* George Antheil. *des.:* Robert Peterson. *ed.:* Viola Lawrence. *players:* Humphrey Bogart, Gloria Grahame, Frank Lovejoy, Jeff Donnell.

INFERNO (1953). *Prod.:* William Bloom. *Dir.:* Roy Baker. *sc.:* Francis Cockrell. *ph.:* Lucien Ballard. Technicolor. *players:* Robert Ryan. Rhonda Fleming, William Lundigan, Henry Hull.

INNOCENTS, THE (1961). *Prod. and Dir.:* Jack Clayton. *sc.:* William Archibald, Truman Capote, John Mortimer. From the novel *The Turn of the Screw* by Henry James. *ph.:* Freddie Francis. *mus.:* Georges Auric. *des.:* Wilfrid Shingleton. *ed.:* James Clark. *players:* Deborah Kerr, Martin Stephens, Pamela Franklin, Megs Jenkins, Michael Redgrave.

IPCRESS FILE, THE (1965). *Prod.:* Harry Saltzman. *Dir.:* Sidney J. Furie. *sc.:* Bill Canaway and James Doran. From the novel by Len Deighton. *ph.:* Otto Heller. Technicolor. *mus.:* John Barry. *des.:* Peter Murton. *ed.:* Peter Hunt. *players:* Michael Caine, Nigel Green, Guy Doleman, Sue Lloyd, Gordon Jackson.

ISLAND OF LOST SOULS, THE (1932). *Dir.:* Erle C. Kenton. *sc.:* Waldemar Young, Philip Wylie. From the novel *The Island of Dr. Moreau* by H. G. Wells. *ph.:* Karl Struss. *players:* Charles Laughton, Bela Lugosi, Richard Arlen, Leila Hyams, Kathleen Burke, Arthur Hohl.

JEOPARDY (1952). *Dir.:* John Sturges. *sc.:* Mel Dinelli. Based on a story by Maurice Zimm. *players:* Barbara Stanwyck, Barry Sullivan, Ralph Meeker, Lee Aaker.

JUNGFRUKÄLLAN (THE VIRGIN SPRING) (1959). *Dir.:* Ingmar Bergman. *sc.:* Ulla Isaksson. Based on a fourteenth-century Swedish legend. *ph.:* Sven Nykvist. *mus.:* Erik Nordgren. *des.:* P. A. Lundgren. *ed.:* Oscar Rosander. *players:* Max von Sydow, Birgitta Valberg, Gunnel Lindblom, Birgitta Pettersson, Axel Düberg, Tor Isedal, Allan Edwall, Ove Porath.

KILLERS, THE (1946). *Prod.:* Mark Hellinger. *Dir.:* Robert Siodmak. *sc.:* Anthony Veiller. From the short story by Ernest Hemingway. *ph.:* Woody Bredell. *players:* Burt Lancaster, Ava Gardner, Edmond O'Brien. The Hemingway story occupies only about five minutes, at the beginning of the film.

KIND HEARTS AND CORONETS (1949). *Prod.:* Michael Balcon. *Dir.:* Robert Hamer. *sc.:* Hamer and John Dighton. *players:* Dennis Price, Valerie Hobson, Alec Guinness.

KUNGSLEDEN (1965). *Dir.:* Gunnar Höglund. *sc.:* Gunnar

Höglund, Bosse Gustafsson. From the novel by Bosse Gustafsson. *ph.:* Bertil Wictorsson. Eastmancolor. *mus.:* Karl-Erik Welin. *players:* Mathias Henrikson, Maude Adelson, Lars Lind, Guy de la Berg.

KWAIDAN (1964). *Prod.:* Shigeru Wakatsuki. *Dir.:* Masaki Kobayashi. *sc.:* Yoko Mizuki. From three stories by Lafcadio Hearn (also known as Yagumo Koizumi). *ph.:* Yoshio Miyajima. Eastmancolor. *mus.:* Toru Takemitsu. *des.:* Shigemasa Toda. *players:* Michiyo Aratama, Misako Watanabe, Rentaro Mikuni, Ganemon Nakamura, Noboru Nakaya, Katsuo Nakamura. The episode referred to in Chapter 8 is entitled *Chawan no naka*, which means "Inside a Teacup". A *chawan* can be used for other liquids than tea, and also for rice; in this case it is used for drinking water.

LADIES MAN, THE (1961). *Prod., dir. and sc.:* Jerry Lewis. Additional material: Bill Richmond. *ph.:* W. Wallace Kelley. Technicolor. *mus.:* Walter Scarf. *des.:* Ross Bella. *ed.:* Stanley Johnson. *players:* Jerry Lewis, Helen Traubel, Pat Stanley, Kathleen Freeman, George Raft, Gloria Jean, Hope Holiday.

LADY FROM SHANGHAI, THE (1947). *Prod., Dir. and sc.:* Orson Welles. Based on a novel by Sherwood King. *ph.:* Charles Lawton. *mus.:* Heinz Roemheld. *des.:* Stephen Goosson, Sturges Carne. *ed.:* Viola Lawrence. *players:* Rita Hayworth, Orson Welles, Everett Sloane, Glenn Anders, Ted de Corsia.

LADY IN A CAGE (1964). *Prod. and sc.:* Luther Davis. *Dir.:* Walter Grauman. *ph.:* Lee Garmes. *mus.:* Paul Glass. *des.:* Hal Pereira, Rudolph Sternad. *ed.:* Leon Barsha. *players:* Olivia de Havilland, Ann Sothern, Jeff Corey, James Caan, Jennifer Billingsley, Rafael Campos. (See

LADYKILLERS, THE (1955). *Prod.:* Michael Balcon. *Dir.:* Alexander Mackendrick. *sc.:* William Rose. *ph.:* Otto Heller. Technicolor. *mus.:* Tristram Cary. *ed.:* Jack Harris. *players:* Alec Guinness, Cecil Parker, Herbert Lom, Peter Sellers, Danny Green, Jack Warner, Katie Johnson.

LEAGUE OF GENTLEMEN, THE (1960). *Prod.:* Michael

Relph. *Dir.:* Basil Dearden. *sc.:* Bryan Forbes. From the novel by John Boland. *ph.:* Arthur Ibbotson. *mus.:* Philip Green. *des.:* Peter Proud. *ed.:* John Guthridge. *players:* Jack Hawkins, Nigel Patrick, Roger Livesey, Richard Attenborough, Bryan Forbes, Kieron Moore, Robert Coote.

LEAVE HER TO HEAVEN (1945). *Prod.:* William A. Bacher. *Dir.:* John M. Stahl. *sc.:* Jo Swerling. Based on the novel by Ben Ames Williams. *ph.:* Leon Shamroy. Technicolor. *players:* Gene Tierney, Cornel Wilde, Jeanne Crain, Vincent Price, Ray Collins, Darryl Hickman.

LITTLE FOXES, THE (1941). *Prod.:* Samuel Goldwyn. *Dir.:* William Wyler. *sc.:* Lillian Hellman, from her own stage play. *ph.:* Gregg Toland. *players:* Bette Davis, Herbert Marshall, Teresa Wright, Dan Duryea.

LONELY VILLA, THE (1909). *Dir.:* D. W. Griffith. *ph.:* G. W. Bitzer, Arthur Marvin. *players:* Mary Pickford, Marion Leonard, Robert Harron, Owen Moore, Adele de Garde.

M. (1931). *Dir.:* Fritz Lang. *sc.:* Thea von Harbou, Lang. *ph.:* Fritz Arno Wagner. Gustav Rabhje, Karl Vash. *des.:* Karl Vollbrecht, Emil Hasler. *players:* Peter Lorre, Ellen Widmann, Inge Landgut, Gustaf Grundgens, Fritz Gnass.

MÉLODIE EN SOUS-SOL (U.K.: **THE BIG SNATCH;** U.S.: **ANY NUMBER CAN WIN**) (1962). *Prod.:* Jacques Bar. *Dir.:* Henri Verneuil. *sc.:* Albert Simonin, Michel Audiard, Henri Verneuil. From the novel *The Big Grab* by John Trinian. *ph.:* Louis Page. *mus.:* Michel Magne. *des.:* Robert Clavel. *ed.:* Françoise Verneuil. *players:* Jean Gabin, Alain Delon, Viviane Romance, Maurice Biraud.

MOBY DICK (1955). *Prod. and Dir.:* John Huston. *sc.:* Ray Bradbury and John Huston. From the novel by Herman Melville. *ph.:* Oswald Morris. Technicolor. (Colour style by Oswald Morris and John Huston.) *mus.:* Philip Stainton. *des.:* Ralph Brinton. *ed.:* Russell Lloyd. *players:* Gregory Peck, Richard Basehart, Leo Genn, James Robertson Justice, Harry Andrews, Bernard Miles, Orson Welles.

MOST DANGEROUS GAME, THE (THE HOUNDS OF ZAROFF) (1932). *Prod. and Dir.:* Ernest Schoedsack, Irving Pichel. *sc.* James Creelman. From a story by Richard Connell. *ph.:* Henry Gerrard. *ed.:* Archie Marshek. *players:* Leslie Banks, Joel McCrea, Fay Wray, Robert Armstrong.

MUSIC BOX, THE (1932). *Prod.:* Hal Roach. *Dir.:* James Parrott. *ph.:* Walter Lundin. *players:* Stan Laurel, Oliver Hardy.

NAKED RUNNER, THE (1967). *Prod.:* Brad Dexter. *Dir.:* Sidney J. Furie. *sc.:* Stanley Mann. Based on the novel by Francis Clifford. *ph.:* Otto Heller. Technicolor. *mus.:* Harry Sukman. *des.:* Peter Proud. *ed.:* Barry Vince. *players:* Frank Sinatra, Peter Vaughan, Derren Nesbitt, Nadia Gray.

NAVIGATOR, THE (1924). *Dir.:* Buster Keaton, Donald Crisp, Jean C. Havez. *sc.:* Joseph A. Mitchell, Clyde Bruckman. *players:* Buster Keaton, Kathryn Maguire, Frederick Vroom, Noble Johnson.

NIGHT HAS A THOUSAND EYES (1948). *Prod.:* Endre Bohem. *Dir.:* John Farrow. *sc.:* Barré Lyndon, Jonathan Latimer. *ph.:* John F. Seitz. *players:* Edward G. Robinson, Gail Russell, John Lund, Virginia Bruce, William Demarest, Richard Webb, Jerome Cowan.

NIGHT OF THE GENERALS, THE (1966). *Prod.:* Sam Spiegel. *Dir.:* Anatole Litvak. *sc.:* Joseph Kessel, Paul Dehn. From the novel by Hans Hellmut Kirst. Based on an incident written by James Hadley Chase. *ph.:* Henri Decaë. Print by Technicolor. *mus.:* Maurice Jarre. *des.:* Alexander Trauner. *ed.:* Alan Osbiston. *players:* Peter O'Toole, Omar Sharif, Tom Courtenay, Donald Pleasence, Joanna Pettet, Philippe Noiret, Charles Gray, Coral Browne, John Gregson, Nigel Stock, Christopher Plummer, Juliette Greco, Yves Brainville, Sacha Pitoëff. The incident mentioned in the credits can be found in the novel *The Wary Transgressor* by James Hadley Chase.

NORTH BY NORTHWEST (1959). *Prod. and dir.:* Alfred Hitchcock. *sc.:* Ernest Lehman. *ph.:* Robert Burks. *mus.:* Bernard Herrmann. *des.:* Robert Boyle. *ed.:* George

Tomasini. *players:* Cary Grant, Eva Marie Saint, James Mason, Jessie Royce Landis, Leo G. Carroll.

NOTTI DI CABIRIA, LE (NIGHTS OF CABIRIA) (1957). *Prod.:* Dino de Laurentis. *Dir.:* Federico Fellini. *sc.:* Fellini, Ennio Flaiano, Tullio Pinelli. *ph.:* Aldo Tonti. *mus.:* Nino Rota. *players:* Giulietta Masina, François Périer, Franca Marzi, Dorian Gray, Amedeo Nazzari.

NOZ W WODZIE (KNIFE IN THE WATER) (1961). *Dir.:* Roman Polanski. *sc.:* Jerzy Skolimowski, Jakub Goldberg, Polanski. *ph.:* Jerzy Lipman. *mus.:* Krzysztof Komeda. *players:* Leon Niemczyk, Jolanta Umecka, Zygmunt Malanowicz.

NUMBER SEVENTEEN (1932). *Prod.:* John Maxwell. *Dir.:* Alfred Hitchcock. *sc.:* Hitchcock, Alma Reville, Rodney Ackland. From the play by Jefferson Farjeon. *ph.:* Jack Cox. *des.:* Wilfred Arnold. *ed.:* A. C. Hammond. *players:* Leon M. Lion, Anne Grey, John Stuart, Donald Calthrop, Barry Jones, Garry Marsh.

ŒIL POUR ŒIL (1957). *Dir.:* André Cayatte. *sc.:* Pierre Bost. From a novel by Vahe Katcha. *ph.:* Christian Matras. Eastmancolor. *players:* Curt Jurgens, Folco Lulli, Paul Frankeur, Dario Moreno, Lea Padovani, Pascale Audret.

ONE TOO EXCITING NIGHT (1912). *Prod.:* Cecil Hepworth.

ORDERS TO KILL (1957). *Dir.:* Anthony Asquith. *sc.:* Paul Dehn. From a story by Donald C. Downes. Adaptation by George St. George. *ph.:* Desmond Dickinson. *ed.:* Gordon Hales. *players:* Paul Massie, Irene Worth, Eddie Albert.

OUTRAGE, THE (1965). *Prod.* A. Ronald Lubin. *Dir.:* Martin Ritt. *sc.:* Michael Kanin. Based on the Japanese film *Rashomon. ph.:* James Wong Howe. *mus.:* Alex North. *des.:* George W. Davis, Tambi Larsen. *ed.:* Frank Santillo. *players:* Paul Newman, Laurence Harvey, Claire Bloom, Edward G. Robinson, William Shatner, Howard Da Silva, Paul Fix.

PARANOIAC (1964). *Prod.:* Anthony Hinds. *Dir.:* Freddie Francis. *sc.:* Jimmy Sangster. *ph.:* Arthur Grant. *mus.:*

Elisabeth Lutyens. *des.:* Don Mingaye. *ed.:* James Needs. *players:* Janette Scott, Oliver Reed, Liliane Brousse, Alexander Davion, Sheila Burrell, Maurice Denham, John Bonney, John Stuart, Colin Tapley, Harold Lang.

PHANTOM OF THE OPERA, THE (1925). *Prod.:* Carl Laemmle. *Dir.:* Rupert Julian. *sc.:* Elliott J. Clawson. Based on the novel by Gaston Leroux. *ph.:* Charles Van Enger. *des.:* Dan Hall. *players:* Lon Chaney, Mary Philbin, Norman Kerry, Snitz Edwards, Gibson Gowland, John Sainpolis, Virginia Pearson.

PLACE IN THE SUN, A (1951). *Prod. and Dir.:* George Stevens. *sc.:* Michael Wilson, Harry Brown. Based on the novel *An American Tragedy* by Theodore Dreiser, and the play by Patrick Kearney adapted from the novel. *ph.:* William C. Mellor. *mus.:* Franz Waxman. *des.:* Hans Dreier, Walter Tyler. *ed.:* William Hornbeck. *players:* Montgomery Clift, Elizabeth Taylor, Shelley Winters, Anne Revere, Raymond Burr.

PLEIN SOLEIL (BLAZING SUN; PURPLE NOON) (1959). *Prod.:* Robert and Raymond Hakim. *Dir.:* René Clément. *sc.:* René Clément and Paul Gégauff. Based on the novel *The Talented Mr. Ripley* by Patricia Highsmith. *ph.:* Henri Decaë. Eastmancolor. *mus.* Nino Rota. *des.:* Paul Bertrand. *ed.:* Françoise Javet. *players:* Alain Delon, Maurice Ronet, Marie Laforêt, Erno Crisa, Frank Latimore.

PUGNI IN TASCA, I (FISTS IN THE POCKET) (1965). *Prod.:* Ezio Passadore. *Dir. and sc.:* Marco Bellocchio. *ph.:* Alberto Marrama. *mus.:* Ennio Morricone. *des.:* Gisella Longo. *players:* Lou Castel, Paola Pitagora, Marino Mase, Liliana Gerace, Pier Luigi Troglio, Jean MacNeil.

PUITS ET LE PENDULE, LE (1963). *Dir.:* Alexandre Astruc. *sc.:* Suzanne Bujot. From the story by Edgar Allan Poe. *ph.:* Nicolas Hayer. *mus.:* Antoine Duhamel. *des.:* André Bakst, Jean-Louis Crozet. *ed.:* Monique Chalmandrier, Sophie Bhaud. *player:* Maurice Ronet. This film was made for television.

RASHOMON (1950). *Prod.:* Jingo Minoru. *Dir.:* Akira

Kurosawa. *sc.:* Shinobu Hashimoto, Kurosawa. From two stories by Ryunosuke Akutagawa. *ph.:* Kazuo Miyagawa. *mus.:* Fumio Hayasaka. *des.:* So Matsuyama. *players:* Toshiro Mifune, Masayuki Mori, Machiko Kyo, Takashi Shimura, Minoru Chiaki, Kichijiro Ueda, Daisuke Kato, Fumiko Homma.

RIDEAU CRAMOISI, LE (THE CRIMSON CURTAIN) (1952). *Prod.:* Sacha Kamenka. *Dir. and sc.:* Alexandre Astruc. From the story by Barbey d'Aurevilly. *ph.:* Eugène Schufftan. *mus.:* Jean-Jacques Grunenwald. *des.:* Mayo. *ed.:* Jean Mitry. *players:* Jean-Claude Pascal, Anouk Aimée, Jim Gerald, Marguerite Garcya.

ROBBERY (1967). *Prod. and Dir.:* Michael Deeley, Stanley Baker. *Dir.:* Peter Yates. *sc.:* Edward Boyd, Yates, George Markstein. *ph.:* Douglas Slocombe. Eastmancolor. *des.:* Michael Seymour. *ed.:* Reginald Beck. *players:* Stanley Baker, Joanna Pettet, James Booth, Frank Finlay, Barry Foster, William Marlowe.

ROBINSON CRUSOE ON MARS (1964). *Prod.:* Aubrey Schenck. *Dir.:* Byron Haskin. *sc.:* Ib Melchior, John Higgins. Based on *Robinson Crusoe* by Daniel Defoe. *ph.:* Winton C. Hoch. Technicolor. *mus.:* Van Cleave. *des.:* Hal Pereira, Arthur Lonergan. *ed.:* Terry Morse. *players:* Paul Mantee, Victor Lundin, Adam West.

ROI SANS DIVERTISSEMENT, UN (1963). *Dir.:* François Leterrier. *sc.:* Jean Giono, from his own novel. *ph.:* Jean Badal. Eastmancolor. *mus.:* Maurice Jarre. *song:* Jacques Brel. *des.:* Philippe Ancellin. *ed.:* Françoise Javet. *players:* Claude Giraud, Charles Vanel, Colette Renard, Pierre Repp, Albert Rémy, René Blanchard.

SAFETY LAST (1923). *Prod.:* Hal Roach. *Dir.:* Fred Newmaker and Sam Taylor. *sc.:* Harold Lloyd, Hal Roach. *ph.:* Walter Lundin. *ed.:* Fred L. Guiol. *players:* Harold Lloyd, Mildred Davies, Bill Strothers, Noah Young, W. B. Clarke.

SALAIRE DE LA PEUR, LE (THE WAGES OF FEAR) (1953). *Dir. and sc.:* Henri-Georges Clouzot. From the novel by Georges Arnaud. *ph.:* Armand Thirard. *mus.:* Georges Auric. *des.:* René Renoux. *players:* Yves Montand, Charles Vanel, Véra Clouzot, Folco Lulli, Peter van Eyck, William Tubbs, P. Centa, Dario Moreno, Jo Dest.

SCARED STIFF (1952). *Prod.:* Hal Wallis. *Dir.:* George Marshall. *sc.:* Herbert Baker, Walter DeLeon. Based on a play by Paul Dickey and Charles W. Goddard. *ph.:* Ernest Laszlo. *mus.:* Leith Stevens. *des.:* Hal Pereira, Franz Bachelin. *players:* Dean Martin, Jerry Lewis, Carmen Miranda, Lizabeth Scott, Dorothy Malone. A previous film of the same story was *The Ghost Breakers* (1940), also directed by Marshall, with Bob Hope and Paulette Goddard.

SCOUNDREL, THE (1935). *Prod., dir. and sc.:* Ben Hecht and Charles McArthur. *ph.:* Lee Garmes. *players:* Noël Coward, Julie Haydon.

SECONDS (1966). *Prod.:* Edward Lewis. *Dir.:* John Frankenheimer. *sc.:* Lewis John Carlino. Based on the novel by David Ely. *ph.:* James Wong Howe. *mus.:* Jerry Goldsmith. *des.:* Ted Haworth. *ed.:* Ferris Webster, David Webster. *players:* Rock Hudson, Salome Jens, John Randolph, Will Geer, Jeff Corey, Richard Anderson.

SERVANT, THE (1963). *Prod.:* Joseph Losey, Norman Priggen. *Dir.:* Joseph Losey. *sc.:* Harold Pinter. From the novel by Robin Maugham. *ph.:* Douglas Slocombe. *mus.:* John Dankworth. *des.:* Richard MacDonald. *players:* Dirk Bogarde, Sarah Miles, James Fox, Wendy Craig, Catherine Lacey, Richard Vernon, Ann Firbank, Doris Knox, Patrick Magee, Jill Melford, Alun Owen, Harold Pinter, Derek Tansley, Brian Phelan, Hazel Terry.

SHANGHAI EXPRESS (1932). *Dir.:* Josef von Sternberg. *sc.:* Jules Furthman. Based on a story by Harry Hervey. *ph.:* Lee Garmes. *des.:* Hans Dreier. *players:* Marlene Dietrich, Clive Brook, Anna May Wong, Warner Oland, Eugene Pallette, Lawrence Grant, Louise Glosser Hale, Gustav von Seyffertitz, Emile Chautard. (See page 45.)

SORRY, WRONG NUMBER (1948). *Prod.:* Hal Wallis and Anatole Litvak. *Dir.:* Anatole Litvak. *sc.:* Lucille Fletcher, based on her own radio play. *ph.:* Sol Polito. *mus.:* Franz Waxman. *players:* Barbara Stanwyck, Burt Lancaster, Ann Richards, Wendell Corey.

SPIRAL STAIRCASE, THE (1945). *Prod.:* Dore Schary. *Dir.:* Robert Siodmak. *sc.:* Mel Dinelli. Based on the novel *Some Must Watch* by Ethel Lina White. *ph.:* Nicholas Musuraca. *mus.:* Roy Webb. *des.:* Albert S. D'Agostino. *ed.:* Harry Marker, Harry Gestad. *players:* Dorothy McGuire, George Brent, Ethel Barrymore, Kent Smith, Rhonda Fleming, Gordon Oliver, Elsa Lanchester, Sara Allgood, Rhys Williams, James Bell.

STRANGE DOOR, THE (1951). *Prod.:* Ted Richmond. *Dir.:* Richard Pevney. *sc.:* Jerry Sackheim. From the story *The Sire de Maletroit's Door* by Robert Louis Stevenson. *ph.:* Irving Glassberg. *mus.:* Joseph Gershenson. *des.:* Bernard Herzburn, Eric Obom. *ed.:* Edward Curtiss. *players:* Charles Laughton, Boris Karloff, Sally Forest, Richard Stapley, Michael Pate, Paul Cavanagh, Alan Napier, William Cottrell.

SUNA NO ONNA (WOMAN OF THE DUNES) (1963) *Prod.:* Kiichi Ichikawa and Tadashi Ohono. *Dir.:* Hiroshi Teshigahara. *sc.:* Kobo Abé. From a novel by Kobo Abé. *ph.:* Hiroshi Segawa. *mus.:* Toru Takemitsu. *ed.:* F. Susui. *players:* Eiji Okada, Kyoko Kishida.

TELL-TALE HEART, THE (1941). *Dir.:* Jules Dassin. *sc.:* Doane Hoag. *ph.:* Paul Vogel. *players:* Joseph Schildkraut, Roman Bohnen, Charles Crowbridge. Other versions of this story by Edgar Allan Poe have been filmed by Desmond Hurst (1934), J. B. Williams (1953, with Stanley Baker as Poe), Ted Parmalee (1953, a UPA cartoon narrated by James Mason), and Ernest Morris (1960).

TESTAMENT DES DR. MABUSE, DAS (1933). *Dir.:* Fritz Lang. *sc.:* Lang and Thea von Harbou. *ph.:* Fritz Arno Wagner. *des.:* Karl Vollbrecht, Emile Hasler. *players:* Rudolf Klein-Rogge, Gustav Diessl, Otto Wernicke, Oscar Beregi.

THEY WON'T FORGET (1937). *Prod.: and Dir.:* Mervyn LeRoy. *sc.:* Robert Rossen. From the novel *Death in the Deep South* by Ward Greene. *ph.:* Arthur Edeson. *mus.:* Adolph Deutsch. *des.:* Robert Haas. *players:* Claude Rains, Gloria Dickson, Edward Norris, Otto Kruger, Allyn Joslyn, Lana Turner.

THIRD MAN, THE (1949). *Prod. and dir.:* Carol Reed. *sc.:* Graham Greene, from his own story. *ph.:* Robert Krasker. *mus.:* zither played by Anton Karas. *des.:* Vincent Korda. *ed.:* Oswald Hafenrichter. *players:* Joseph Cotten, Trevor Howard, Alida Valli, Orson Welles.

THIRTY-NINE STEPS, THE (1935). *Dir.:* Alfred Hitchcock. *sc.:* Charles Bennett and Ian Hay. Based on the novel by John Buchan. *ph.:* Bernard Knowles. *players:* Robert Donat, Madeleine Carroll, Godfrey Tearle.

TRAVERSÉE DE PARIS, LA (PIG ACROSS PARIS) (1956). *Dir.:* Claude Autant-Lara. *sc.:* Jean Aurenche, Pierre Bost. From the story by Marcel Aymé. *ph.:* Jacques Matteau. *mus.:* René Cloerec. *des.:* Max Douy. *ed.:* Madeleine Gug. *players:* Jean Gabin, Bourvil, Jeanette Batti, Louis de Funès.

VERDICT, THE (1946). *Prod.:* William Jacobs. *Dir.:* Don Siegel. *sc.:* Peter Milne. From the novel *The Big Bow Mystery* by Israel Zangwill. *ph.:* Ernest Haller. *mus.:* Frederick Hollander. *ed.:* Thomas Reilly. *players:* Sydney Greenstreet, Peter Lorre, Joan Lorring, George Coulouris, Rosalind Ivan, Paul Cavanagh, Arthur Shields, Morton Lowry.

WARNING SHOT (1966). *Prod. and dir.:* Buzz Kulik. *sc.:* Mann Rubin. Based on the novel *711—Officer Needs Help* by Whit Masterson. *ph.:* Joseph Biroc. *special photographic effects:* Paul K. Lerpae. Technicolor. *mus.:* Jerry Goldsmith. *des.:* Hal Pereira, Roland Anderson. *ed.:* Archie Marshek. *players:* David Janssen, Ed Begley, Keenan Wynn, Sam Wanamaker, Lillian Gish, Stefanie Powers, Eleanor Parker, George Grizzard, George Sanders, Steve Allen, Joan Collins, Walter Pidgeon, John Garfield Jnr.

WINDOW IN LONDON, A (1940). *Prod.:* Josef Somlo. *Dir.:* Herbert Mason. *sc.:* Ian Dalrymple, B. Cooper, *ph.:* Glen McWilliams. *mus.:* Bretton Byrd. *des.:* Ralph Brinton. *ed.:* Philip Charlot. *players:* Michael Redgrave, Sally Gray, Paul Lukas, Hartley Power, Patricia Roc.